Margin Tips
Shopping tips, historical facts, handy hints, and invaluable information on activities to help visitors to make the most of their time in Las Vegas.

Feature Boxes
Notable topics are highlighted in these special boxes.

Key Facts Box
This box gives details of the distance covered on the tour, plus an estimate of how long it should take. It also states where the tour starts and finishes, and gives key travel information such as which days are best to do the tour or handy transport tips.

Footers
Those on the left-hand page give the itinerary name, plus, where relevant, a map reference; those on the right-hand page show the main attraction on the double page.

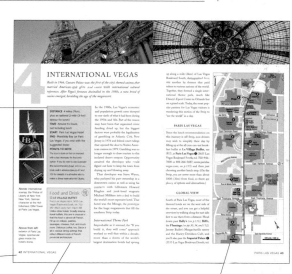

Food and Drink
Recommendations of where to stop for refreshment are given in these boxes. The numbers prior to each restaurant/café name link to references in the main text. On city maps, restaurants are plotted.

The $ signs at the end of each entry reflect the approximate cost of a two-course meal for one, with a glass of house wine. These should be seen as a guide only. Price ranges, also quoted on the inside back flap for easy reference, are as follows:

$$$$	$60 and above
$$$	$40–60
$$	$20–40
$	$20 and below

Route Map
Detailed cartography shows the itinerary clearly plotted with numbered dots. For more detailed mapping, see the pull-out map, which is tucked inside the back cover.

ART ENTHUSIASTS

Tour 3 focuses on the city's main fine arts attractions such as the 18B Arts District and Wynn Las Vegas (also tour 8). Out in the Valley of Fire (tour 14) are stunning, ancient petroglyphs.

RECOMMENDED TOURS FOR...

DAREDEVILS

Tour 6 is designed for adrenalin junkies, but you might also try the Skywalk at Grand Canyon West (tour 15) and some target practice at the Gun Store (tour 9).

OUTDOOR TYPES

Go horseback riding at Red Rock Canyon (tour 11) or pick one of the hiking trails in the Valley of Fire or off the Northshore Road (tour 14), or around Lake Las Vegas (tour 10).

CHILDREN

Attractions such as Circus Circus and *Star Trek – The Experience* (tour 5) as well as Shark Reef and MGM Lions (tour 2) are sure to keep the kids happy. Even a ride on the monorail (tour 6) is lots of fun.

GAMBLERS

It's hard to come to Vegas and not get bitten by the gambling bug. Tour 12 gives a lowdown on the games, but you can also check out the Lost Vegas Gambling Museum and Shop (tour 1), and cheap-and-cheerful Slots a Fun (tour 13).

☀ INSIGHT GUIDES

LAS VEGAS
Step by Step

Discovery
CHANNEL

APA PUBLICATIONS L
Part of the Langenscheidt Publishing Group

CONTENTS

Introduction
About this Book 4
Recommended Tours 6

Orientation
Overview 10
Food and Drink 14
Shopping 16
Gambling 18
Weddings 20
The Movies 22
History: Key Dates 24

Walks and Tours
1. Classic Las Vegas 28
2. All-Natural Vegas 32
3. Artistic Las Vegas 36
4. International Vegas 42
5. Las Vegas with Kids 48
6. Thrill-seekers' Vegas 52
7. Ladies-only Vegas 56
8. Gay Las Vegas 60
9. Vegas for the Boys 65
10. Romantic Las Vegas 68
11. Old West Las Vegas 72
12. Gamblers' Las Vegas 78
13. Budget Las Vegas 86
14. Lake Mead and
    the Valley of Fire 90
15. Hoover Dam and
    Grand Canyon West 93

Directory
A–Z of Practical
  Information 98
Accommodations 110
Restaurants 118

Credits and Index
Picture Credits 124
Index 126

ABOUT THIS BOOK

Above: neon Las Vegas.

This *Step by Step Guide* has been produced by the editors of Insight Guides, whose books have set the standard for visual travel guides since 1970. With top-quality photography and authoritative recommendations, this guidebook brings you the very best of Las Vegas in a series of 15 tailor-made tours.

WALKS AND TOURS

The tours in the book provide something to suit all tastes, budgets, and available time. As well as covering Las Vegas's classic attractions, there are suggestions for thrill-seekers, visitors traveling with children, romantics, and, of course, gamblers, as well as for those who want to venture beyond the city limits.

We recommend that you read the whole of a tour before setting out. This should help you to familiarize yourself with the tour and enable you to plan where to stop for refreshments – options for this are shown in the "Food and Drink" boxes, which are recognizable by the knife and fork sign, on most pages.

ORIENTATION

The tours are set in context by this introductory section, giving an overview of the city plus the lowdown on subjects such as food and drink, shopping, getting married in Vegas, and the city in the movies. A succinct history timeline in this chapter highlights the key events that have shaped the city.

DIRECTORY

Also supporting the tours is the Directory chapter, comprizing a user-friendly, clearly organized A–Z of practical information, our pick of where to stay in the city, and select restaurant listings; these eateries complement the cafés and restaurants that feature within the walks and tours themselves and are intended to offer a wider choice.

The Author

Formerly a Las Vegas attorney, Richard Harris left practice in 1982 to pursue a career in travel writing and publishing. He has since worked as managing editor for John Muir Publications (now Avalon Travel), as editor for Ulysses Press and Globe Pequot Press, and as contributing editor for Birnbaum Guides, Access Guides and Fodor's Guides. He is the author or co-author of 38 travel guidebooks for the aforementioned publishers as well as John Wiley & Sons, VIA Books/AAA and Gibbs Smith, Publisher, and has contributed chapters to the Insight Guides to Colorado and Utah. He specializes in writing about the American West, Mexico, Central America, and the Caribbean. He has served for many terms as president of the New Mexico Book Association and is a past president of PEN New Mexico, a chapter of the international writers' rights organization founded by Katherine Galsworthy and George Bernard Shaw. When not traveling, he lives in Santa Fe, New Mexico, with his Australian cattle dog, Remington.

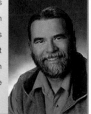

HEDONISTS

What is your pleasure? Perhaps relaxing by the pool (tours 1 and 8), being pampered in a spa (tours 7 and 10), or just letting someone else do the hard work as you lie back in a gondola (tour 15).

NATURE LOVERS

Get back to nature at the Las Vegas Natural History Museum (tour 11), gaze upon White Tigers, lions, sharks, and dolphins (tour 2), or explore the Botanical Gardens that are part of what's on offer at Ethel M's Chocolate Factory (tour 10).

HISTORY HUNTERS

Beneath the glitz are reminders of an interesting past. Pioneer-era destinations include the Nevada State Museum (tour 11), while the Flamingo (tour 1) is where "Bugsy" Siegel started it all.

FOODIES

Fine dining options are suggested in the Food and Drink boxes in tours 3 and 4. Chocolate lovers should visit Ethel's Chocolate Lounge (tour 7).

MUSEUM BUFFS

It may be a surprise to find that Las Vegas has a wide range of museums, from the Marjorie Barrick Museum and Arboretum (tour 2), to the Liberace Museum (tour 8), and the Lost City Museum (tour 14).

ORIENTATION

An overview of Las Vegas's geography, customs, and culture, plus illuminating background information on food and drink, shopping, gambling, quickie weddings, the movies, and history.

OVERVIEW	10
FOOD AND DRINK	14
SHOPPING	16
GAMBLING	18
WEDDINGS	20
THE MOVIES	22
HISTORY: KEY DATES	24

OVERVIEW

If you haven't visited Las Vegas lately, you're in for a revelation. Formerly a notorious den of iniquity, where gambling reigned supreme, "Sin City" has been transformed over the last decade or so into a giant, multi-billion-dollar adult amusement park.

Above: gold is the color of choice for casino decoration; locals Downtown; typical temptation.

Las Vegas attracts 37 million visitors a year, making it one of the most popular tourist destinations on earth. It started with gambling and made a name for itself in the quickie wedding business, but neither of those is the main draw for visitors today. Warm winters, excellent dining and shopping, the world's largest resort hotels, fine arts, great golf, and championship sporting events – and, of course, the biggest names in stage entertainment – make for an exciting mix that even nongamblers can't resist.

THE STRIP

When most people think of Las Vegas, the part they usually have in mind is the four-mile (6km) stretch of Las Vegas Boulevard South known as the Strip, which is lined with America's biggest and most famous casino resorts. Oddly enough, the Strip is not officially part of Las Vegas. Ever since development began there in the 1930s, property owners along the Strip, keen to avoid local taxation and regulation (and originally to stay outside of local police jurisdiction), have successfully blocked all attempts to annex it into municipal Las Vegas or establish it as a separate town, and it remains an unincorporated area of Clark County.

The center of the action along the Strip has moved over the years. Resort development originally started around the intersection with Flamingo Road and moved south past Desert Inn Road to Sahara Avenue. When the themed megaresort boom came in the 1990s, construction moved south, spanning from Flamingo Road to Tropicana Avenue and into the under-developed land past Tropicana. Now this area has been built up to near capacity, and most of the older hotels along the northern part of the Strip have been razed to make way for new, even more ambitious projects.

Today, from the Fashion Show Mall north, most property has been consolidated into a few hugely ambitious multiple-use projects, combining resort hotels, condominium complexes, and retail space. These include Echelon Place, Project CityCenter, and the twin-towered Trump International, all presently under construction and slated for completion between 2009 and 2011 at costs of billions of dollars apiece.

OFF-STRIP

Large resort hotels have also been built within a mile or two east and west of the Strip. The trend started in 1969

with the building of the International Hotel near the original Las Vegas Convention Center, east of the north end of the Strip. The International would become famed as the concert venue of such top Vegas headliners as Elvis Presley, Liberace, and Barbra Streisand. Later, as the convention center expanded to become one of the largest in America, the International was replaced by the Las Vegas Hilton, the largest of several business-class hotels along Paradise Road and Convention Center Drive.

More recent off-Strip resort development has focused on two areas near the southern Strip. Across Interstate 25, West Flamingo Road is the site of several major high-rise resorts including the Rio Suites and the Palms, site of a number of top nightclubs, and the city's newest large concert venue.

To the east, along Paradise Road between the Strip and the University of Nevada – Las Vegas campus, major resorts include the hip Hard Rock Hotel and the well-appointed non-gaming Alexis Park Resort.

Las Vegas is the fastest-growing city in the US, so new residential areas spring up seemingly overnight. Since completion of a new freeway linking it with McCarren International Airport and the Strip area, the formerly one-horse, magnesium-mining town of Henderson south-east of Las Vegas has boomed into a sprawling bedroom community of more than a quarter of a million people, displacing Reno as Nevada's second-largest city. Henderson also has numerous casino resorts, from budget options such as the Fiesta to the luxurious Green Valley Ranch Resort and Spa.

Above from far left: chancing Lady Luck; entrance tickets; dancing shoes; neon is everywhere in Vegas.

Left: photographed in 1969, these Folies Bergère showgirls at the Tropicana are dressing for a show celebrating the centennial of the original, Paris-based, dance troupe. Of the showgirls' distinctively sexy wiggle, producer Donn Arden once said, "If you twist right and swing that torso, you get a revolve going in there that's just right. It isn't the way a woman should walk necessarily – unless she's a hooker."

Above from far left: Slots a Fun and Circus Circus; biker gear in the desert, just outside Vegas.

DOWNTOWN

Formerly nicknamed "Glitter Gulch" until city fathers tried to shed its dubious reputation by renaming it "the Fremont Street Experience," Fremont Street is the center of the action in Downtown Las Vegas. Many serious gamblers prefer Downtown casinos for their lack of touristic distractions. The five-block pedestrians-only section of Fremont has ten casino hotels, a single somewhat sleazy but historic striptease joint, and the world's largest LED screen, four blocks long and 90ft (27m) above the street, where the spectacular, free Viva Vision extravaganzas are shown nightly. To the west,

a run-down area on the edge of Downtown is being redeveloped as the 18b Arts District, a studio and gallery zone that comes to life with big street celebrations twice a month (see p.38).

AROUND THE CITY

As you will see if you fly into Las Vegas during daylight hours, the metropolitan area is surrounded by a vast, unpopulated desert, the Mojave. To the east, and hidden from the city by a jagged, barren mountain range, lies Lake Mead, created during the 1930s by damming the confluence of the Colorado and Virgin rivers. Near the Henderson entrance to Lake Mead National Recreation Area, the much smaller, similarly manmade Lake Las Vegas has condominiums, a golf course, and several luxury resort hotels.

To the south-west stand the Spring Mountains, with the stately 11,916-ft (3,632-m) Mt. Charleston as their centerpiece. Here, Las Vegas visitors are often amazed to find evergreen forests and alpine wilderness covered with snow more than half the year. The mountainside has a ski area and a small, rustic year-round hotel, the Mt. Charleston Inn.

CLIMATE

Due to its desert location, Las Vegas has an extremely dry climate. The average annual rainfall is a scant, unpredictable 4 inches (10cm), with no more than half-an-inch (1cm) falling in any single month. Summer temper-

---

Water Attraction

In an arid desert, Las Vegas's fast growth and the importance to tourism of water attractions such as huge, elaborate pools and the Bellagio's fountains have created a water crisis. The newly opened Las Vegas Springs Preserve (333 South Valley View Boulevard; tel: 702-822-7736; www.lvspringspreserve.org; daily 10am–10pm; charge) is a multimillion-dollar effort to educate the public about water conservation with interactive exhibits, demonstration gardens and even a simulated flash flood. It also

features a re-creation of the original springs that brought explorers and ranchers to the valley, as well as an arboretum of plants from the various North American deserts and 2 miles (3km) of hiking trails through the natural Mojave landscape. Great for kids!

atures are hot, with typical daytime highs of 100–106°F (38–41°C). However, as most activities take place in air-conditioned comfort, Las Vegas is a year-round tourist destination with no noticeable low-season slump. Winter low temperatures hardly ever dip below freezing, with daytime highs usually in the 60s and 70s (16–26°C). Because the humidity is too low to hold much heat, at all times of year the temperature drops by about 30°F (17°C) when the sun goes down.

PEOPLE

Fifty per cent of Las Vegas residents are of European ancestry, 28.6 per cent are of Latin American ancestry, and 11.3 per cent are black. Asians, though accounting for a mere 4.8 per cent of the population, are the city's fastest-growing minority group. Only 0.7 per cent of Las Vegas residents are American Indians. About 19 per cent of the people who live in Las Vegas are legal immigrants to the States, though only one-third of them have become naturalized US citizens.

As of 2005, the US Census Bureau reports, the median household income for the greater Las Vegas area was $49,169, about 6 per cent above the national average. But the per capita income was only $22,060, or 34 per cent below the national average. This apparent contradiction is explained by Las Vegas's young population, with an extraordinarily large percentage of children and teens who are not part of the work-force and a large percentage of two-income families.

Above: vest from Vegas; the monorail.

Below: city views, with the Stratosphere Tower to the left and the mountains behind.

FOOD AND DRINK

In an earlier era, Las Vegas was known for 99-cent breakfasts and ridiculously cheap all-you-can-eat buffets, but times have changed. Today on the Strip, you're always within a few minutes' walk of a 200-dollar dinner.

The 1992 opening of Wolfgang Puck's first Vegas location, Spago, in Caesars Palace, proved that upscale restaurants could draw capacity crowds in casino resorts. The knock-on effect is that food quality has improved in all levels of eateries. Now hotel coffee shops serve gourmet breakfasts and casino buffets have been transformed into smörgåsbords of international cuisine. There is even a fast-food restaurant that offers 60-dollar Kobe beef burgers.

Dining on a Budget

Eating on a tight budget in Vegas isn't as easy as it used to be, but it's still possible. Look for buffets and coffee shops in the older hotels on the Strip, such as the Sahara, Flamingo, and Riviera, or head towards Downtown, where food and lodging cost much less. Check out unique budget dining options listed in this book, such as Tiffany's in White Cross Drug *(see p.29)* and the San Francisco Shrimp Bar Downtown in the Golden Gate *(see p.88).*

WHERE TO EAT

Every large resort has restaurants – some as many as 15 of them – in every price range. These range from no-frills coffee shops to luxe eateries. You might expect the patrons at the celebrity-chef signature restaurants found in every major resort to be high rollers on winning streaks, but most serious gamblers seem to prefer buffets. Big-name, big-price restaurants thrive because of lovers' trysts, family reunions, and all the many occasions for making a vacation as unforgettable as possible, never mind the expense.

Global Choice

Since Las Vegas has no regional cuisine of its own, most of its restaurants feature international menus representing one country or another. For instance, Paris Las Vegas has French restaurants including an elegant dining room midway up the Eiffel Tower and an upscale room filled with the paintings of Pablo Picasso and decorated by his son. Other hotels offer great Italian, Japanese, and Mexican restaurants – as well as the ubiquitous steakhouse and seafood place. If you choose to venture off the Strip, you'll find everything from Argentinean, Greek, and Indian cuisine to Irish pub grub.

Themed Affairs and Shows

Theme restaurants have proliferated in Vegas. Local versions of the Hard Rock Café and the Harley-Davidson Café pull in brisk business, and then there are international themed places, from the imposing Hofbrauhaus to a rainforest eatery complete with thunderstorms.

A few dinner shows also exist, ranging from the family-oriented *Tournament of Kings* at the Excalibur to *The Sopranos' Last Supper*, an audience-participation show celebrating a different kind of "family," at the Empire Ballroom.

Bountiful Buffets

Casinos still have buffets, but many of them have been transformed from the cheap eats cafeterias of old into lavish spreads featuring foods from around the world as well as prime rib, shrimp, and crab. Despite the improvement of the city's culinary landscape as a whole, buffets can still be a hit-and-miss affair, but the Rio's Carnival World Buffet is a cut above. No longer as affordable as they once were, most all-you-can-eat buffets cost $20 to $30, though some in older hotels still charge less than $10.

EATING HOURS

Las Vegas may be open all night, but most of its restaurants are not. Many upscale and midrange restaurants only serve dinner from about 5pm to 10 or 11pm during the week and an hour later at weekends. Buffets usually operate from 7am until 10 or 11pm, often closing briefly between breakfast, lunch, and dinner service. However, virtually all casinos have a coffee shop that serves food 24 hours a day.

BEVERAGES

Alcohol fits right into the Sin City image, and it's common to see people staggering along the Strip in various states of inebriation any time of the day or night. If you're someone whose idea of a great vacation involves way too much drinking, you're in the right place. In fact, if you're gambling in a casino – even slowly for low stakes – waitresses will keep bringing you drinks compliments of the house. The reason is simple: casino managers know that the more you drink, the more money you will lose. In the end, it costs less to gamble sober and pay for your drinks.

Penalties for Excess

Things change outside the casino. Drunken pedestrians are tolerated, but statistically, Las Vegas is one of the highest-risk cities in the US for alcohol-related traffic accidents, so the local police take driving under the influence very seriously. There are "sobriety checkpoints" all over town, and the ubiquitous patrol cars seem to spend most of their time breathalyzing erratic drivers. Drivers who test over 0.8 per cent blood-alcohol content are likely to spend the night in jail, post bond the next day, and return to Vegas months later to stand trial. First-time drunk driving offenses are punished by mandatory jail sentences.

Above from far left: buffet at Paris Las Vegas; French pâtisserie; tender all-American steaks; peach cocktail.

Reservations
If you plan to dine at any resort restaurants other than buffets or coffee shops, make reservations as soon as possible after you check in, bearing in mind that literally thousands of other resort guests may also be expecting to eat there. And if you have your eye on a top-of-the-line signature restaurant, it's wise to call for reservations several weeks in advance.

SHOPPING

Although locals often complain that "real world" shopping in Las Vegas is dominated by mundane places like Wal-Mart and Target, there is no question that the Strip has become one of America's top upscale shopping zones, rivaling Beverly Hills' Rodeo Drive and Palm Beach's Worth Avenue.

Above: luggage, shoes, and kitsch Beatles souvenirs.

Late Opening
Fancy a spot of shopping before bedtime? Some of the malls located inside casinos stay open as late as midnight.

Not so long ago, shopping possibilities in Las Vegas were so dismal that many locals drove 300 miles to Los Angeles for whatever they couldn't buy at their neighborhood convenience store. The ruling powers believed that spending in stores competed with losing money in the casinos. But then a few resorts, such as the original MGM Grand, opened small, expensive shopping areas where players who got lucky in the casinos could spend their winnings – or spouses could spend while their partners gambled. In the 1990s, exclusive boutiques, shops, and designer outlets proliferated until today many visitors bypass gambling altogether, preferring to spend their time at the fantastic malls.

STRIP SHOPPING

Most large casino resorts now have shopping zones. Some, such as the stores in Circus Circus and the Excalibur, are oriented toward families and children. Others are essentially department store-size versions of standard hotel gift shops, specializing in swimwear and items bearing the hotel logo.

Retail Fantasies

The best of the resort shopping malls are truly spectacular. Don't miss the atmospheric malls at theme hotels, such as Paris Las Vegas's Le Boulevard, the Venetian's Grand Canal Shoppes, or the Via Bellagio, at the hotel of the same name. The Wynn Esplanade is so exclusive that its retailers include a Ferrari-Maserati dealership. The Miracle Mile Shops at the new Planet Hollywood (formerly the Aladdin) has no fewer than 170 sleek, trendy stores, but the long-established Forum Shops in Caesars Palace still reigns supreme in the realm of ultra-expensive designer boutiques.

Shopping Mecca

With its center-Strip location, the huge, upscale Fashion Show Mall *(see pp.57 and 61)* was expanded in 2003 to nearly three times its original size – it now has more than 200 stores and restaurants – making it one of the largest shopping malls in the US. It is also the only one that is anchored by locations of all six of the country's top-quality department store chains – Bloomingdales, Macy's, Dillards, Nordstrom, Neiman Marcus, and Saks Fifth Avenue.

BEYOND THE STRIP

Most visitors find it unnecessary to leave the Strip to indulge their wildest

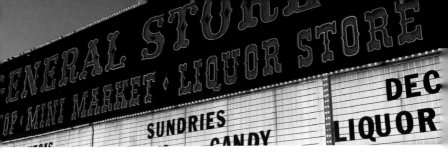

shopping fantasies. Off-Strip possibilities are rather limited. For instance, the much-anticipated Downtown mall Neonopolis has developed into an entertainment complex of restaurants, night clubs, a huge video arcade, and a 14-screen movie theater, fringed with novelty shops.

Malls off the Strip

Of the several malls that have sprung up to serve the burgeoning eastern suburbs, The Boulevard, located about five miles (8km) from the Strip at 3528 South Maryland Parkway, is the largest. While it has about the same number of retail stores as the Fashion Store Mall, The Boulevard covers a larger area – 1.2 million sq ft (111,484 sq m) – and so claims the distinction of being Nevada's largest mall. Many of the stores here are the same ones as you'll find in every major shopping mall in America.

A unique Las Vegas shopping experience, Chinatown Plaza at 4255 Spring Mountain Road is the largest collection of Asian retail stores and restaurants in the state. The mall was created to accommodate Hong Kong businesspeople seeking to relocate to the US during the 1990s, when Hong Kong came under Chinese rule. Its success has come largely from the growing numbers of Chinese and other Asian visitors who come to Las Vegas each year. Besides an Asian supermarket and numerous gift shops, you will find a Chinese bookstore, a medicinal herb shop, and a jewelry store that specializes in jade.

Outlet Opportunities

Downtown also has a relatively new outlet store complex, Las Vegas Premium Outlets, with shops such as Ann Taylor, Eddie Bauer, Guess, Armani Exchange, Bose, and Polo Ralph Lauren offering savings of 25 to 65 per cent off regular list prices.

Many outlet store buffs also make excursions across the desert to Fashion Outlets of Las Vegas, located 40 miles (64km) south on I-15 (Exit 1) in the town of Primm. While many of the 100 stores here are the same as those in Las Vegas Premium outlets, the atmosphere is more relaxing, and the remote location makes it a fun trip.

Above from far left: Las Vegas glass souvenirs; all and sundry at the General Store.

Below: a successful shopping trip.

GAMBLING

There is one sure-fire way to make money from a casino: buy one. If you play the slots, tables, or sports books in Las Vegas, do it to have fun. The golden rule for happy gambling is setting a limit beforehand and not exceeding it. Quit while you're ahead, too. For our gambling tour, see pp.78–85.

Above: all set: chips, a game, and the dice.

You may have Lady Luck on your side when you play, but then again you may not. Serious players pre-calculate a stake range – highest to lowest bet – by multiplying the number of hours they intend to play by the number of games per hour, and dividing their "bankroll" by the result, to set a maximum stake. A low stake is then set at around 20 per cent of the maximum, or less. Low bets are made until a winning streak is hit, then stakes are progressively raised. This way, losses are kept small and winnings are maximized.

It's a good idea to ride a winning streak. If you strike it lucky, put a profit to one side, then raise your stakes and go for it. If you start to lose, cut back or – better still – walk away. Playing comfortably low stakes offers more fun in the long run. Betting $5 one hundred times and winning some of the time gives more hours of entertainment than playing $500 and maybe losing, once.

BLACKJACK

Blackjack offers some of the best odds in the casino. The house's natural edge is between 3 and 5 per cent, and skilled players can narrow that to 0.5 per cent with betting and playing combinations. The object is to get a hand of cards closer to 21 than the dealer. Cards take their numerical value, except for face cards counting as 10, and aces, which the player can value as one or 11. The top hand, an ace with a 10 or a picture, makes 21 – "blackjack."

Blackjack deals are usually from a six- or eight-deck plastic "shoe." Some – mostly downtown – casinos play with a single deck, giving the player much better chances to predict the remaining cards but payouts are usually lower.

CRAPS

A craps game may look daunting, but is really fairly simple. It also offers good odds to players; the house edge on a simple "pass line" bet is only 1.4 per cent. Bets are made for and against a dice roll, called "right" or "wrong" bets. The dice pass around the table. No-one has to roll, but the thrower must bet on his own game.

At the first, or "come out" roll, a throw of 2, 3, or 12 is known as craps. This is a win for bets on the "don't pass" line, or wrong bets. The numbers 7 or 11 are automatic winners for "pass-line" right bets. Any other number rolled establishes the shooter's "point." The aim then is to roll the point again before hitting a 7.

KENO

Keno is hugely popular because it is so simple to play, and a $50,000 payout is possible on a $1 bet. All you need do is pick some numbers on a ticket and wait. It's easy, and it's fun. It's also among the lowest player odds in the house, with a casino edge of 20 to 30 per cent.

Due to a mystery of Nevada gaming regulation, Keno is not, technically, a lottery. Pay-outs must be collected immediately after each game, and before the next game starts, or they are forfeited. Take a place at the bar or café and call a Keno runner over, pick your lucky numbers and wait for the draw. Any number of tickets can be bought for each game, and there are endless combinations to mark the numbers, which the runner will happily show you. If the runner returns with winnings, it is polite to tip.

ROULETTE

The wheel spins, the ball spins against it. The ball drops, and clatters. It bounces once, twice, and comes to rest in number 7. The dealer places the white marker next to your chip on the 7, and your $100 bet is joined by $3,500 in chips.

Or not. Pay out can be a dizzying 35 to 1, but the 0 and 00 make the odds 37 to 1 against your predicting the correct number. If the ball falls on 0 or 00, all bets lose, save for those predicting that exact outcome. This makes the overall house edge 5.26 per cent, and about the poorest table odds in town.

The safest bets on the wheel are the outsiders; the "dozens" (first 12, second 12, third 12, or one of the three "columns"), which pay out 2 to 1. Otherwise, 1 to 1 payouts are offered by "red or black," "odd or even," or "first or last 18."

SPORTS BOOKS

In the Sports Book, players back their expertise in predicting sports events. Odds are offered on football, baseball, Indy car races, and championship boxing. But the main event in the book is horse racing, still the largest spectator sport in the US. A horse's previous performance, or "form," is a guide, and the simple bets – "win" or "place" – are the most profitable.

POKER

The ability to read other players at the table can be as important in poker as getting the best cards. Players who think they have the strongest hand will try to lure money into the "pot," but players who believe they have weaker cards may bluff, to scare others out of the game. Poker is the only game where play is against other gamblers and not against the house. Instead, the house gets a cut – usually around 5 per cent – off the top of each pot.

A common form of poker in Vegas is Texas Hold 'em. Each player is dealt two cards, face down. Through progressive betting rounds, five "community cards" are dealt, face up. Each player then makes the highest five-card hand they can from the seven cards available.

Professional Advice
Serious and professional players consider whatever is in front of them as their own money – not the house's – and safeguard their chips accordingly. The house plays most games with what seem like relatively small odds. Over time, though, the odds will most likely attract your bankroll across the table. The main thing your skill can do is to slow the roll.

WEDDINGS

Las Vegas is a favorite destination not only for gambling and conventions, but also as a mecca of matrimony, a paradise of promises, a Valhalla for vows. Over 174,000 troths are pledged here every single year.

Vegas originally became a wedding capital because only in Nevada could you get a marriage license without a blood test and a waiting period. Today, only a handful of states require either one so the only real advantage to getting married in Las Vegas is that you can get a wedding license in the middle of the night.

STATISTICS

Vegas has around 50 wedding chapels, which open daily from 8am to midnight (24 hours on legal holidays) from gimmicky drive-throughs to graceful, dignified wedding chapels. There are also elegant wedding gardens and most major resorts on the Strip have their own wedding chapels too.

The invitation to impulsiveness is taken advantage of by an average of 337 couples every day, though over Valentine's Day weekend as many as 2,000 are married. At least 87,000 marriage licenses, each costing $55, are issued each year. Some legal I.D. is required, such as a driver's license, passport, or birth certificate.

CELEBRITY WEDDINGS

Celebrity weddings have been fashionable in Sin City since silent-film stars Clara Bow and Rex Bell chose to tie the knot here.

The Golden Years

Perhaps the first marriage that grabbed the public's attention took place in 1943, when Betty Grable and trumpeter and band leader Harry James exchanged their vows at the Little Church of the West. The *Las Vegas Review-Journal* reported that more than 100 locals left their beds in the middle of the night to make a trip to the train station, hoping to get a glimpse of Grable as she waited for James to return from Mexico with his divorce papers. The

Below: Vegas-style chapel, complete with drive-up wedding window, flower shop, and the facility to rent tuxedos and gowns.

wedding took place just before dawn, and, after the ceremony, the couple drove back to Los Angeles.

Mickey Rooney married Ava Gardner at the same spot in January, 1942. Over the next three decades he made seven return trips to the same chapel, concluding with a marriage to January Chamberlin in 1978.

Among other famous marriages at that busy chapel was that of Zsa Zsa Gabor and actor George Sanders in 1949. In the same year, Rita Hayworth married singer Dick Haymes at the Sands and on July 19, 1966 Ol' Blue Eyes married Mia Farrow at the Sands, Sinatra's second home for nearly a decade.

Ongoing Trend

The trend for quickie Vegas-style nuptials looks set to continue. Billy Bob Thornton married Angelina Jolie in 2000 at the Little Church of the West, and in January 2004, Britney Spears married Jason Allen Alexander at the Little White Chapel; the marriage was famously annulled 50 hours later.

THEMED NUPTIALS

It is the extreme and themed nuptials for which Las Vegas is most famous. Viva Las Vegas Wedding Chapel at the northern end of the Strip offers a Blue Hawaiian wedding named after the Elvis movie, as well as a pink Cadillac wedding, an intergalactic wedding and a Woodstock wedding.

The Excalibur provides a medieval-themed ceremony and the MGM

Grand offers Merlin the wizard to officiate while a fire-breathing dragon attempts to thwart the nuptials. The Las Vegas Hilton provides Intergalactic Federation regalia and hires *Star Trek* characters as witnesses. Betrothals can be made by, with, or even to the *Phantom of the Opera*. Other options include a beach party, a Wild West wedding on horseback, a pirate ship, the Las Vegas Motor Speedway, the bottom of the Grand Canyon, under water, and the top of Paris Las Vegas's Eiffel Tower.

EXTREME WEDDINGS

Those with a taste for the extreme can marry on a bungee jump, during a roller-coaster ride or, for even whiter knuckles, during a parachute-jump or sky-dive. Ceremonies can be officiated in a helicopter hovering over the Strip, the Grand Canyon, or the Hoover Dam. For more serene mid-air marriages, a hot-air balloon is available with a basket large enough for bride, groom, and the assembled company.

ON FOUR WHEELS

One wedding chapel offers a drive-through venue, so the bride and groom don't even need to leave their car. For the more up-market autophile, you can have a limousine drive to the scenic backdrop of your choice – and get married in the back of the stretch. In fact, a few limos come equipped with whirlpools and hot tubs, so the happy couple can bubble and betroth simultaneously.

Above from far left: just like Elvis and Priscilla; cherubs in the mood for love.

Wedding Outfits Catering to Vegas's wedding market are numerous bride stores. These include I&A Formalwear (3345 South Decatur Boulevard; tel: 702-364-5777) and Bridal de Paris (2207 Las Vegas Boulevard South; tel: 702-301 1002), where packages include hair, makeup, and clothes for the bride, bridesmaids, and mother of the bride.

THE MOVIES

The gold and the glitter, the instant flips of fortune, and the fantasy façades of Vegas also offer endlessly rich plot potential and terrific locations. All this has kept Sin City in the movies and in the business of movies. The fact that Hollywood is just a short hop in a private jet away helps, too.

Nevada on Screen
In 1960, both Marilyn Monroe and Clark Gable played their last movie roles in John Huston's *The Misfits*, much of it filmed in the Nevada desert. Arthur Miller's script about a disillusioned divorcée was uncannily prophetic of the Monroe-Miller marriage.

From the days of silent films, Las Vegas had starring roles in movies such as *The Hazards of Helen* and John Ford's 1932 film *Airmail*. Edwin L. Mann's 1946 film *Lady Luck* was a moral tale about the irresistible lure of gambling. *Ocean's 11*, made in 1960, was the famous Rat Pack saga, directed by Lewis Milestone and shot when Frank Sinatra, Dean Martin, Sammy Davis Jr, and Peter Lawford could spare time from carousing. The film was remade in 2001 with George Clooney, Brad Pitt, Matt Damon, and Julia Roberts topping a stellar bill, and featured several interiors shot in the Bellagio.

Elvis Presley wooed Ann-Margret from the Sahara on the Strip all the way to Lake Mead and Mount Charleston in *Viva Las Vegas* (1964); the famous pairing was rumored to be mirrored off screen. In 1971 Sean Connery went Downtown to Fremont Street as James Bond in *Diamonds Are Forever*, which critic Leonard Maltin described as a "colorful comic book adventure."

SCIENCE FICTION

Vegas has served as the backdrop for cheesy sci-fi movies as well. In *The Amazing Colossal Man* (1957) Las Vegas came under attack from an Army officer who grew 60ft (18m) tall after surviving an atomic explosion, but the assault came from elsewhere in Tim Burton's wild 1996 sci-fi fantasy, *Mars Attacks*, in which the Strip was spectacularly demolished. In the same year, the special effects were about the only stars of *Independence Day* to survive with reputations intact.

Rick Moranis reprised his goofy scientist role from *Honey, I Shrunk the Kids* in *Honey, I Blew Up the Kid* (1992), where his two-year-old son becomes 150ft (46m) high and grows even larger when he comes near electricity.

GANGSTER MOVIES

The Mob has received a lot of attention in celluloid. In 1972 and 1974, parts 1 and 2 of Francis Ford Coppola's *The Godfather* trilogy were partly filmed and set locally. The saga of the Corleone family includes references to the Mob's attempts at legitimacy in the Nevada gaming business.

Warren Beatty played a highly romanticized Benjamin "Bugsy" Siegel while conducting an on-screen romance with his soon-to-be wife Annette Bening in Barry Levinson's *Bugsy* in 1991. Martin Scorsese's *Casino* (1995), starring Robert de Niro and Sharon

Stone, is a brutally comic tale of mobsters hustling their way into the casino business, much of it filmed in the Strip's Riviera casino. *Get Carter*, the classic British gangster movie made in 1971, was remade in 2000, set in Vegas and Seattle, and starred Sylvester Stallone.

AN EASY BACKDROP

Many top movies have used Vegas as a ready-made setting, or even as a plot device. Dustin Hoffman won an Oscar for his role in *Rain Man* in 1988, which co-starred Tom Cruise and featured a scene filmed in the Pompeiian Fantasy Suite of Caesars Palace.

Johnny Depp took narcotics aplenty and trashed a hotel room as a reporter covering a prosecutors' war-on-drugs convention in the 1998 film of Hunter S. Thompson's *Fear and Loathing in Las Vegas*, filmed partly in the Riviera, Circus Circus, and Stardust hotels.

Actor Nicolas Cage is a virtual Vegas veteran, having starred in several local movies: the 1992 comedy *Honeymoon in Vegas* that features the Bally's Casino Resort and the Excalibur; the dark 1995 drama *Leaving Las Vegas*; two years later, *Con Air*; and the following year, *Snake Eyes*. In 2007 he starred as a Vegas-based clairvoyant in the movie *Next*.

Vince Vaughn and Jon Favreau spent a weekend womanizing in Vegas – specifically, outside the Stardust and inside the Fremont downtown – in the 1996 indy surprise hit, *Swingers*. Favreau returned to the scene in 1998 with the much darker *Very Bad Things*, on the worst that can happen in Vegas.

ONGOING INTEREST

It was the 2001 remake of *Ocean's Eleven* that really unleashed a rush of interest in using Las Vegas as the glamorous backdrop to a number of films and television programmes. Since then, William H. Macy played the unluckiest man alive in *The Cooler*, a gritty, violent, yet charming meditation on the nature of luck in old-time Vegas. For his role as a mobbed-up casino boss in the show, Alec Baldwin was nominated for both an Oscar and a Golden Globe for Best Supporting Actor in 2004. And Drew Barrymore and Robert Duvall starred in *Lucky You* (2007), that dealt with the pitfalls of high-stakes gambling.

The Nevada Film Office assists hundreds of films, music videos, and multimedia productions on a daily basis and barely a week goes by without one of the networks shooting in town. It is fitting, then, that one of these, CBS, really hit the jackpot with *CSI: Las Vegas*, which is one of the most successful TV series of recent years. And let's not forget NBC's hit series *Las Vegas*, now in its fifth season, though without series star James Caan.

Above from far left: the Rat Pack made two films together, the original *Ocean's 11* and the poor follow up *Robin and the Seven Hoods;* James Bond only made one trip to Vegas, in *Diamonds are Forever*; George Clooney heads a stellar cast in the remake of *Ocean's 11* (for the original shot of this scene, from the 1960 film, *see pp.26–7*) William H. Macy's character in *The Cooler* has the handy ability to ruin other gamblers' good runs.

Film Critics Society

Every year since 1997, the Las Vegas Film Critics Society has presented its Sierra Awards in 19 categories and issued a list of the year's top 10 films. Made up of print, media, TV and Internet critics from the Las Vegas area, at time of printing the society had 11 members.

HISTORY: KEY DATES

Barely 100 years old, Las Vegas has always had a pioneering spirit. A magnet for stars and celebrities, it has one of the most colorful histories of all US cities, one which is played out against a backdrop of constant transformation.

John C. Fremont
On May 13 1844 the best-known explorer in the US, John C. Fremont, led an overland expedition west. He elected to camp at Las Vegas Springs, and recorded the spot on his map. A legend was born, and Fremont was – and is – remembered in Downtown's main thoroughfare, Fremont Street.

EARLY HISTORY

11,000 B.C. Paleo-Indians first hunt big game in the cool, lush Las Vegas Valley.
A.D. 1150 Paiute Indians begin to winter in the Las Vegas Valley.
1829 Mexican trader Antonio Armijo camps near desert springs and names the area Las Vegas (the meadows).
1844 Noted explorer John C. Fremont, leading an overland expedition, camps at a site that as a tribute to him years later becomes known as Fremont Street, in downtown Las Vegas.

PIONEER YEARS

1848 US acquires the region by treaty after winning the Mexican War.
1855–7 Mormons found a settlement in Las Vegas to convert the Paiutes.
1902 San Pedro, Los Angeles, and Salt Lake City Railroad (later known as Union Pacific) buys land and lays out Las Vegas.

Right: the Sultan of Swing, Frank Sinatra, and harem, in 1955.

| 1908 | Telephone and water lines are established in the region. |
| 1911 | The city of Las Vegas is incorporated on March 16. |

GOLDEN AGE

1920	The first Vegas gaming hall, the Northern Club, is opened in Downtown's Fremont Street.
1931	Gambling in Nevada is legalized.
1935	President Franklin D. Roosevelt dedicates Hoover Dam.
1945	Mobster Benjamin "Bugsy" Siegel opens the Flamingo Hotel, attracting Hollywood stars to Las Vegas.
1955	Las Vegas's first high-rise hotel, the nine-story Riviera, is built.
1960	The Rat Pack comes to town.
1966	Reclusive millionaire Howard Hughes moves into a penthouse on top of the Desert Inn and opens six casinos.

MODERN LAS VEGAS

1989	The Mirage casino opens with 3,039 rooms
1990	Las Vegas's population reaches 258,295, doubling in just a decade.
1992	The success of Warren Beatty's movie *Bugsy* prompts the Flamingo Hilton to open the Bugsy Celebrity Theater.
1993	The MGM Grand opens as the world's biggest resort.
1995	The Fremont Street Experience opens. Gaming revenues are $5.7 billion, 78 per cent of the US total.
1997	New York-New York, a scaled-down version of Manhattan, opens.
1998	The Bellagio, the world's most expensive hotel ($1.7 billion), opens.
1999	Paris Las Vegas opens.
2000	The Venetian opens. Vegas now has 19 of the world's 20 biggest hotels.

21ST CENTURY

2002	Nevada is named the fastest-growing state in the US.
2003	Roy (of Siegfred & Roy) is badly mauled by one of the pair's tigers, and the act is forced to close.
2004	The Harrah's group buys historic casino Binion's Horseshoe from the Binion family. In July, the long-awaited monorail opens.
2005	Steve Wynn's eponymous Wynn Las Vegas opens.
2007	The Stardust is demolished to make way for Echelon Place, a $4 billion mega-resort due for completion in 2010. The New Frontier is demolished.

Above from far left:
Mormons preaching in the wilderness, 1853; Marlene Dietrich, pictured here in 1953, was a frequent guest and performer in Vegas.

Hotel Rates
According to the *New York Times*, in 1953 a first-class hotel in Vegas charged $7.50 a night, while a motel charged $3.

WALKS AND TOURS

1. Classic Las Vegas   28
2. All-Natural Vegas   32
3. Artistic Las Vegas   36
4. International Vegas   42
5. Las Vegas with Kids   48
6. Thrill-seekers'
    Las Vegas   52
7. Ladies-only Vegas   56
8. Gay Las Vegas   60
9. Vegas for the Boys   65
10. Romantic Las Vegas   68
11. Old West Las Vegas   72
12. Gamblers' Las Vegas   78
13. Budget Las Vegas   86
14. Lake Mead and
    the Valley of Fire   90
15. Hoover Dam and
    Grand Canyon West   93

CLASSIC LAS VEGAS

From the late 1940s to the mid-1970s, Las Vegas's mix of high life and low life made it unique in the annals of American pop culture. While visitors today find little to remind them of that era, nostalgia buffs who search for it can still discover traces of old-time Vegas.

Further Reading
Check out Janice Oberling's *Haunted Nevada* that deals with ghostly sightings of deceased Las Vegas legends such as Bugsy Siegel, Elvis Presley, and Red Foxx. The book's accounts inspired Robert Allen's "Haunted Vegas" bus tours (Sat–Thur at 9pm; tel: 702-737-5540; www.haunted vegastours.com) that leave from the Greek Isles Hotel *(see p.31).*

DISTANCE 12 miles (19km)

TIME 10.5 hours (including dinner and a show)

START Fremont Street

END Greek Isles Hotel

POINTS TO NOTE

This route can be done by car, taxi, or CAT bus routes 108 and 117. Order tickets for *The Rat Pack Is Back* well in advance, especially if going on a Saturday (there are no performances on Friday), if you choose to continue the tour into the evening.

One of America's youngest cities, Las Vegas, nonetheless, has quite a past, and this tour provides the ideal way to discover it. The route takes you from the area known as Downtown, where it all started, to what could arguably be described as *the* classic Vegas hotel, to an evening show that will transport you back to the good old days of the Rat Pack.

If you haven't already had breakfast, and are coming from the Strip, we recommend you set yourself up for the day with breakfast at **Tiffany's Café**, see ⒒①.

Right: the covered Fremont Street.

DOWNTOWN

Fremont Street

At the northern end of the Strip is Downtown, where gambling started in Las Vegas. Its main thoroughfare is **Fremont Street ❶**. If it's not too hot – which it may be in summer despite the shade afforded by the vaulted projection screen 90ft (27m) above street level – stroll up the five-block pedestrians-only section of the street.

Despite attempts to make it super-respectable, Downtown still has more old-time flavor than the Strip: look out for classic neon signs such as Vegas Vic and Vegas Vickie; spin a slot machine at Binion's Gambling Hall, founded in 1947 by legendary Texas bootlegger and convicted murderer Benny Binion, chief rival of the mobsters who built the Strip around the same time; and sip a cold drink at the Fremont, where Wayne "Mr. Vegas" Newton made his singing debut in 1959.

Here, too, is the now-posh Golden Nugget, where billionaire hotel developer Steve Wynn got his start in the days when Downtown was dusty, disreputable, and sleazy.

In the morning, the street is an easygoing place, where you can relax over coffee in a streetside café, then wander up to the renewed Fremont East Historic District around Neonopolis for a look at the outdoor Neon Museum's collection of old-time signs. After dark it becomes the Fremont Street Experience, featuring the world's largest light show *(see p.89)* and live entertainment on two stages, all free.

Lost Vegas Gambling Museum

Don't miss the **Lost Vegas Gambling Museum and Shop**, in **Neonopolis ❷** (450 Fremont Street, tel: 702-385-1883; daily 10am–8pm; charge). This small commercial museum features Bugsy Siegel memorabilia and historic photos of old-time casino hotels being imploded to make way for the "new" Strip, plus vintage casino chips, ashtrays, matchbooks, and swizzle sticks.

Allow time to browse around the Neonopolis shopping mall/entertainment complex. If you drive, note that Neonopolis has a parking fee.

At this point in the tour it should be around lunchtime and a good time to take a break. As the tour continues by heading up the Strip, a good option en route is the **Peppermill Inn**, see 🍴❷.

Above from far left: dazzling neon in Fremont Street; cowgirl; cowboy; bold sign for the Riviera.

Food and Drink 🍴

① TIFFANY'S CAFÉ
White Cross Drugstore, 1700 Las Vegas Boulevard South; tel: 702-380-7711; daily 24hr; $
Inexpensive breakfasts any time of the day or night used to be a Vegas hallmark. Today, one of the last places to find one is this old-time Greek-American lunch counter. It opened in the 1950s as the Liberty Café and is today an artists' hangout, located midway between Downtown and the central Strip.

② PEPPERMILL INN
2895 Las Vegas Boulevard South; tel: 702-735-4177; daily 24hr; $
Breakfast, lunch, dinner or late-night snack, you'll always find huge portions at this cozy restaurant and lounge nestled next to the towering Riviera casino hotel near the north end of the Strip. Entrées range from cheeseburgers and fries to Chilean sea bass. A restaurant since 1972, the Peppermill is rumored to have been a mobsters' meeting place in the old days. It is better known as a location for the 1995 movie *Casino*; Robert De Niro is said to have liked the place so much that he continued to eat here after filming was completed – and still does when in town.

THE FLAMINGO

Continue by heading south up the Strip to the **Flamingo ❸** (3555 Las Vegas Boulevard South, tel: 702-733-3111/888-902-9929; www.flamingolv. com; *see also pp.34 and 112*), the casino hotel that started it all.

Opened by mobster Benjamin "Bugsy" Siegel in 1946 as part of a money-laundering scheme, the hotel has been renovated beyond recognition by subsequent owners including Kirk Kerkorian and the Hilton Corporation, but you can still find a bronze plaque commemorating Siegel in the outdoor garden of the hotel's wedding chapel.

It is the only site in Las Vegas that formally acknowledges the organized crime ties of the city's past. (Mayor Oscar Goodman, a former criminal lawyer who once represented Siegel's boss, mob financier Meyer Lansky, has proposed a Mob Museum dedicated to the city's shady past, but most developers of the "new" Las Vegas oppose the idea.)

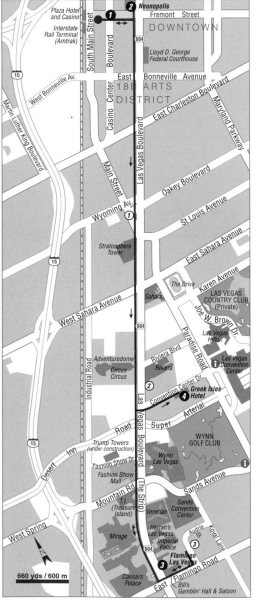

Food and Drink 🍴

③ BATTISTA'S HOLE IN THE WALL

4041 Audrie Street; tel: 702-732-1424; www.battistasvegas.com; daily 5–10:30pm; $$–$$$

Run by the same family for more than 30 years, this atmospheric Italian restaurant has walls covered with historic photos of its many celebrity patrons. All entrées come with soup or salad, house wine, garlic bread, and cappuccino. Reservations advised.

RAT PACK SHOW

If you want to continue the themed tour into the evening, our suggestion is an early dinner at **Battista's Hole in the Wall**, see ⑪③, just behind the Flamingo, on Audrie Street, followed by a classic show, *The Rat Pack is Back*.

The show plays at the **Greek Isles Hotel ❹** (305 Convention Center Drive, tel: 702-952-8000; www.greek islesvegas.com; shows Sat–Thur 8:15pm; *see also p.116*), back up the Strip (going north, turn right on to Convention Center Drive after Wynn Las Vegas.)

This impersonator show reincarnates Frank Sinatra and his "Rat Pack" members, Dean Martin, Sammy Davis Jr., and Joey Bishop, who often performed together in the 1960s and became the era's most renowned Las Vegas celebrities. The gang are sent back from heaven (presumably) to "do it one more time" in Vegas. Conspicuously absent is fellow Rat Packer Peter Lawford, who as J.F. Kennedy's brother-in-law severed his ties with the group so that Sinatra's alleged Mafia connections would not embarrass the President. The show ends at around 10:30pm.

Above from far left: glitzy Golden Nugget; the Flamingo; ol' Blue Eyes; The Rat Pack.

Elvis Impersonators

Perhaps the biggest Las Vegas celebrity of all time (in more ways than one), Elvis Presley has inspired more "tribute performers" (impersonators) than any other celebrity in history. In Vegas, impersonators have become such a cliché that professional Elvis tribute shows are fewer than they once were, though you'll still come across costumed Elvises on the street, and many wedding chapels offer ceremonies conducted by Elvis lookalikes. You can see a bronze statue of The King in the Las Vegas Hilton (3000 South Paradise Road; tel: 702-732-5111), which stands on the site of the old International Hotel where Elvis played 837 sold-out shows. Or, at Bill's Gamblin' Hall (3595 Las Vegas Boulevard South; tel: 702-737-2100), you may be able to catch a show by Big Elvis, the sometime 900-lb (408kg) entertainer, who has been known to take sabbaticals in order to lose weight. But the place wannabe Elvises most often congregate to see and be seen, in the hope of becoming the next star of the casino's long-running *Spirit of the King* lounge show, is Fitzgerald's Casino (200 East Fremont Street; tel: 702-385-3232; www.fremontcasino.com).

ALL-NATURAL VEGAS

Las Vegas residents have a saying: "There's nature all over this town – human nature." Yet in fact, animal lovers will find a number of big-budget exhibits that most zoos would envy, as well as some beautiful indoor gardens.

Spectacular Show
The artificial volcano in front of the Mirage "erupts" on the hour from sundown to midnight, sending smoke and flames 100ft (30.5m) in the air. Fueled by natural gas, it has nozzles that emit a piña colada-scented mist that conceals the odor of the gas.

DISTANCE 6 miles (10km)
TIME Around 8.5 hours
START/END The Mirage
POINTS TO NOTE
All the sights on this tour except those at the university and also the lunch recommendation are within walking distance. However, the CAT bus route 202 serves both the university and the Long Life Vege. This tour is a good one to do with children, if they are animal lovers.

It is, perhaps, ironic that a city such as Vegas that is so thoroughly artificial has so successfully managed to exploit some of nature's most dramatic protagonists, such as tigers, sharks, and lions. The fact that it has done so in its unforgiving desert location is truly impressive.

THE MIRAGE

Begin the tour at the **Mirage ❶** (3400 Las Vegas Boulevard South; tel: 791-7111 or 800-929-1111; www.mirage.

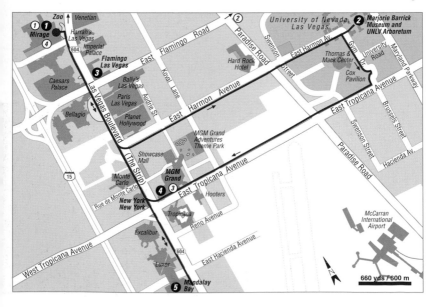

com; *see also pp.44 and 110)*, on the Strip. The inspiration for the array of widely emulated "theme" hotels on the Las Vegas Strip, the Mirage was the most expensive hotel ever built, costing $630 million in 1989.

It was the venue for Siegfried & Roy's animal magic show from 1990 to 2003, when the duo retired after Roy Horn was injured by a white tiger during their act. A larger-than-life statue of the duo and one of their tigers stands in front of the hotel. The Mirage was completely remodeled in 2005–6 to emphasize its exotic tropical nature theme. Guest rooms are luxurious, though somewhat small by modern Las Vegas standards.

You might like to start with an early (9am) breakfast at the hotel's casual **Caribe Café**, see ⑪①. After breakfast, take a look at the impressive, 53-ft (16-m) long, 20,000-gallon (75,700-l) salt-water **aquarium** (daily 24hr; free) by the front desk that is home to 60 species of fish from the South Pacific Ocean and the Caribbean Sea.

Siegfried and Roy's Secret Garden and Dolphin Habitat

At the end of the shopping promenade is this open-air jungle area (Mon– Fri 11am–5.30pm; Sat, Sun 10am–5.30pm; summer: daily 10am–7pm; charge) with waterfalls and a pool. The area is home to 40 rare or endangered species including Siegfried & Roy's white tigers and a white lion.

The white tigers, which live in conditions modeled after their natural habitat, are descendants of a breeding pair donated to a North American zoo by the Maharaja of Rewa, India, in 1958. They are not a distinct species, but the result of the appearance of a rare recessive gene.

A larger pool with windows for underwater viewing is home to bottlenose dolphins, which are not trained to perform tricks but are provided with toys to play with on their own.

Tropical Rainforest

Also in the Mirage, by the front entrance under a 100ft-high (31m)

Above from far left: underwater tunnel for excellent viewing; tiger at the Secret Garden; rainforest in the Mirage; sharks at Mandalay Bay's Shark Reef.

Above: Siegfried, Roy, and one of their big cats, immortalized in bronze by the front of the Mirage.

Below: the Mirage.

Food and Drink 🍴
① CARIBE CAFÉ

Mirage Hotel, 3400 Las Vegas Boulevard South; tel: 702-791-7111 or 800-374-9634; daily 24hr; $$
Tropical flowers decorate the tables in this casual café within the Mirage. The excellent breakfast options include eggs Benedict, pancakes, waffles, and the house specialty: a filling omelet cooked with ranchero salsa, Monterey Jack cheese, guacamole, and refried beans. Also does all-American sandwiches and good seafood dishes.

Above: at Mandalay Bay's Shark Reef.

Las Vegas Zoo
Can't get enough animal viewing? Las Vegas does have a small zoo, the Southern Nevada Zoological and Botanical Park, located about 15 minutes' drive north-west of the Strip (1775 Rancho Drive; tel: 702-647-4685; charge). Besides every species of poisonous reptile that lives in Nevada, the zoo's biggest draw is the only family of Barbary apes in the US.

glass dome, a lush indoor garden (daily 24hr; free) with waterfalls, pools, and bridges contains more than 100 species of tropical plants, including hundreds of orchids and bromeliads along the walkways. The misty, humid atmosphere makes for a wonderful contrast to the dry desert heat outside.

MARJORIE BARRICK MUSEUM AND ARBORETUM

At around noon, take a taxi or drive to the **Marjorie Barrick Museum and UNLV Arboretum ❷** (4505 South Maryland Parkway; tel: 702-895-1421; http://hrcweb.nevada.edu/Museum; Mon–Fri 8am–4:45pm, Sat, Sun 10am–2pm; free), which focuses on the flora and fauna of the Mojave Desert that surrounds the city.

The museum is centrally located on the campus of the University of Nevada – Las Vegas (UNLV), which lies around 2 miles (3km) east of the Strip. If driving, the simplest way to get there from the Mirage is to drive south on the Strip for about one mile (2km) to East Harmon Avenue, which ends in the middle of the campus, turning south at Gym Drive. The museum is right there. The building's entrance features a fascinating xeric garden of drought-resistant plants, both local and from other desert areas around the world. Inside are exhibits on Nevada's birds and live reptiles, as well as dioramas, fossils, and artifacts created by the American Indians of the Southwest, as well as those from ancient Mexico.

UNLV Arboretum

The university's "arboretum" is a series of gardens throughout the campus, including native plant collections as well as a rose garden, an Aids memorial garden, and a pool designed to attract birds, with a shaded viewing area.

Lunch

By now it should be around 2pm. If you fancy lunch, a good option for healthy eating is the **Long Life Vege**, see ⑪②, around a mile (2km) east of the UNLV campus on East Flamingo Road. After lunch, return to the Strip by driving directly west along East Flamingo Road.

If you do not want to stop for refreshment at this point, head straight back to the Strip by continuing south on Gym Drive to East Tropicana Avenue, and turning right; this brings you to the Strip where it meets **New York New York** *(see pp.46, 88, and 115)*, at no. 3790.

FLAMINGO WILDLIFE HABITAT

The route now continues by exploring nature attractions at a number of other large casino hotels, starting with the modest, beautifully landscaped island off the main lobby of the **Flamingo Las Vegas ❸** (3555 Las Vegas Boulevard South; tel: 702-733-3111; www.flamingolv.com; *see also pp.30 and 112*). This island is home to a flock of Chilean flamingos, as well as numerous Asian pheasants, swans, ducks, parrots, turtles, and koi.

MGM LIONS

After about 30 minutes at the Flamingo, stroll three long blocks south along the Strip to the MGM **Lion Habitat** at the MGM **Grand** ❹ (3799 Las Vegas Boulevard South, tel: 702-891-1111; www.mgmgrand.com; daily 11am–10pm; free; *see also pp.50 and 114*).

The lion habitat is near the hotel entrance and the **Rainforest Café**, see ⑪③. Here, you can see descendants of the original lion from MGM studios' opening logo on display in a glass-domed, three-level enclosure with a transparent tunnel that lets spectators walk through the habitat in safety. Lions are rotated twice daily, spending most of their time on cat wrangler Keith Evans's ranch 12 miles (19km) outside the city. A fee is charged for photography.

MANDALAY BAY SHARK REEF

If the lions have given you a taste for sharp-toothed carnivores, **Shark Reef** at the **Mandalay Bay Hotel** ❺ (3950 Las Vegas Boulevard South; tel: 702-632-7777; www.mandalaybay.com; daily 10am–11pm; charge; *see also pp.46, 70, and 114*) should appeal. To get there, continue for another two blocks south, where the Mandalay Bay Hotel's 22-ft (7-m) deep aquarium is one of the largest in the US, with 1½ million gallons (5½ million litres) of salt water. The desert setting makes it extra spectacular.

The aquarium contains some 1,200 fish species, including 15 kinds of sharks, from the tiny Port Jackson shark to the fearsome nurse shark, in the main tank, along with manta rays and sea turtles. Other exhibits include endangered golden crocodiles and Amazon predators including piranhas, leaping monkey fish, and red-tailed catfish, which can swallow a duck whole. Transparent tunnels take you through the underwater world, while audio wands provide narration, and naturalists are on hand to answer questions.

To bring the tour full circle, consider heading back to the Mirage for dinner at **Cravings**, see ⑪④, which does one of the better all-you-can-eat buffets on the Strip.

Above from far left: at Shark Reef; early artwork at the Marjorie Barrick Museum; ape at Las Vegas zoo; ray at Shark Reef.

Food and Drink

② LONG LIFE VEGE
4130 Sandhill Road; tel: 702-436-4488; daily 11am–9.30pm; $$
Located in a small shopping center a mile (2km) or so east of the UNLV campus on Flamingo Road, this friendly, health-conscious restaurant serves vegan Chinese food, as well as a few seafood selections.

③ RAINFOREST CAFÉ
MGM Grand, 3799 Las Vegas Boulevard South; tel: 702-891-8580; Sun–Thur 8am–11pm, Fri–Sat 8am–midnight; $$
Kids love this jungle-shrouded restaurant with its waterfalls, artificial trees, and animatronic gorillas and elephants. As if it weren't hard enough to carry on a conversation over the shrill and roaring animal noises, simulated thunderstorms with lightning flashes and misty rain take place every half-hour. The large, predictable family dining menu features cute names – Safari Salads, Passport to Paradise Pizza, Galapagos Seafood Pasta, Congo Catfish, and so on. Desserts include a Sparkling Volcano brownie sundae big enough for two kids (or about six adults) to share.

④ CRAVINGS
The Mirage, 3400 Las Vegas Boulevard South; tel: 702-791-7111 or 800-374-9634; weekdays 7am–10pm, weekends 8am–10pm; $$$
Revamped in 2004 by world-renowned designer Adam Tihany, Cravings features 11 cooking stations and a gourmet spread of international cuisine. Expect a long wait in line.

ARTISTIC LAS VEGAS

Until recently, Las Vegas was notoriously lacking in cultural sophistication. While there is still little of the performing arts, paintings are another matter and the city is emerging as one of the top art destinations in the Southwest.

DISTANCE 7 miles (11km) to the 18b Arts District and back
TIME Around 4 hours (allow extra time if you are also doing breakfast, dinner, and a show)
START/END The Venetian
POINTS TO NOTE

Reservations are advisable for breakfast at Bouchon and must be made far in advance for dinner at Picasso, if you choose to eat there. Tickets should be purchased in advance for any of the hotel art exhibits, as well as for seats at *Le Rêve*. This tour is best done by car or taxi.

Timing
Art buffs should plan their Las Vegas visit for the first Friday of the month, if at all possible, in order to take in the big monthly celebration in the 18b Arts District.

Food and Drink
① BOUCHON
Venetian Hotel, 3355 Las Vegas Boulevard South; tel: 702-414-6200; www.venetian.com; daily 7–10:30am, 5–11pm; weekends only 11:30am–3pm, oyster bar daily 3–11pm; $$$
This French bistro at the top of the Venezia Tower, with an alfresco dining area surrounded by gardens as well as an indoor picture-window area, is ranked by many food critics as one of the finest casual gourmet restaurants in America. Diners can savor bistro classics including *Poulet Rôti* (roast chicken) and *fruits de mer* (seafood) but breakfast here is much more affordable, and the ambience is the same. Breakfast items range from a basket of French pastries to an elaborate version of baked eggs Florentine over wilted spinach with *jambon au poivre* (peppered ham) and *boulangère* potatoes simmered in beef-onion stock. Besides the usual breakfast juices and beverages, you can order fresh strawberry milk or an espresso martini.

When in 1998, billionaire developer Steve Wynn announced that he would display works from his world-class art collection in his elegant new hotel, the Bellagio *(see pp.40 and 112)* – and charge admission to see them – other casino owners scoffed. The displays, though, were an immediate hit, and, because they were only open to hotel guests, drew the wealthiest clientele on the Strip. Today, the thoroughfare has no fewer than three major art museums, and galleries and artists' studios have proliferated throughout the city.

THE VENETIAN

We suggest starting with an early breakfast at the Bouchon, see ⑪①, in the **Venetian ❶** (3355 Las Vegas Boulevard South; tel: 702-414-6200; www.venetian.com; *see also p.111)*. This should set you up nicely for a stroll along the **Grand Canal** (Sun–Thur 10am–11pm, Fri–Sat 10am–midnight), the Venetian's shopping zone, with its *trompe-l'oeil* sky fresco, detailed building façades, singing gondoliers, and strolling vendors and street performers, which all seems a world apart from the Las Vegas glitz outside.

Of special interest to art connoisseurs, the **Regis Galerie** (tel: 702- 414-3637; www.regisgalerie.com) carries Fabergé

eggs, tabletop bronze sculptures, gemstone globes, *giclées* (high-tech reproductions) and more. Also of note is the **Bernard K. Passman Gallery** (tel: 702-791-3376; www.passman.com), which displays works by the sculptor, now in his 90s, who is best known for his works in black Caribbean coral.

Guggenheim-Hermitage Museum

The next stop, still within the Venetian, is the **Guggenheim-Hermitage Museum** (tel: 702-414-2440; www. guggenheimlasvegas.org; daily 9:30am–7:30pm; charge). Opened in 2001, this 7,660sq-ft (712sq-m) exhibition hall remains the most prestigious art museum in Las Vegas. It is a joint project of the Solomon R. Guggenheim Foundation, operators of the Guggenheim Museums in New York City, Venice, Berlin, and Bilbao, and the Russian Ministry of Culture, supervisor of the Hermitage Museum in the former Imperial Winter Palace in St. Petersburg, Russia.

The Las Vegas museum does not have a permanent collection of its own but displays instead temporary exhibits of works from the New York and

Above from far left: inspecting the artworks at the Guggenheim; artistic ceiling at the Venetian.

Above: carefully crafted glass *(top);* valuable artwork on display at the Wynn Las Vegas *(bottom).*

Left: the Venetian.

Above from left: four scenes from the 18b Arts District.

Above: art lovers at exhibitions in the 18b Arts District.

Russian Guggenheim and Hermitage museums respectively, which change every three to nine months. Recent exhibits have included the imaginative ("Robert Mapplethorpe and the Classical Tradition," a side-by-side comparison of the photographer's works with those of the 16th-century Flemish Mannerists), the fully comprehensive ("Treasures from the Guggenheim and Hermitage Collections: Picasso, Monet, and More"), the historical ("The Majesty of the Tsars: Treasures from the Kremlin Museum"), and the lighthearted ("The Pursuit of Pleasure," images of leisure in 16th- to 20th-century European art).

18B ARTS DISTRICT

By now it should be around 1pm. If you're hungry, taxi or drive down the Strip to Charleston Boulevard. A lunch option here is **Tinoco's Bistro**, see ⑪②. After a bite to eat, it is time to explore the other side of the Las Vegas arts scene, at the **18b Arts District**. (Readjust your schedule if you are fortunate enough to be in town for the district's First Friday or third Sat festivities – *see right*.)

The 18b Arts District got its name when the city declared this run-down 18-block area between the Strip and Downtown to be its official art studio zone. Still dominated by car repair shops and used furniture stores, it doesn't look like much unless you know which doors to peek behind – except during the monthly event, **First Friday**. This sees all the studios in the district throw open their doors for receptions and other local artists display in the streets, and has become a major celebration, attracting as many as 15,000 visitors between 6 and 9pm. A new festival, **ArtAbout**, held on the third Saturday of each month from 2pm till 10pm, includes not only studio receptions but also street performers, children's activities, and a farmers' market.

Arts Factory

At other times of the month, highlights of the arts district include the **Arts Factory** ② (101–7 East Charleston Boulevard, tel: 702-676-1111; www.theartsfactory.com; hours vary: call or visit website for details). The *de facto* center of this creative melting pot, this old brick warehouse with its exterior mural commemorating the city gay and lesbian community appears abandoned until you enter through the black westside door and go upstairs. Here, you'll find around 15 small studios that share space with a graphic arts firm and an architect.

S2 Art Group

Another highlight of this area is the **S2 Art Group** ③ (1 East Charleston

Food and Drink

② TINOCO'S BISTRO

103 East Charleston Boulevard; tel: 702-464-5008; www.tinocos.net; Mon–Fri 11am–3pm, Mon–Sat 5–10pm; $$
As artsy as you could wish for with its distressed wood floor and walls covered with modern paintings, this untouristy restaurant on the ground floor of the Arts Factory offers luncheon choices that range from wild mushroom and lobster pasta to chicken marsala to Chilean sea bass.

Boulevard; tel: 702-868-7880; hours vary: call or visit www.s2art.com for details). The former lithographer for Norman Rockwell, Jack Solomon, moved his studio in 1991 from New York to Las Vegas, where several artists use his flatbed presses, and you can often watch them at work in this storefront space next to the Arts Factory.

Other Commercial Galleries

Also in the 18b Arts District, **Dust Gallery 4** (1221 South Main Street; tel: 702-880-3878; www.dustgallery. com; Wed–Sat noon–5pm) represents local and national painters and sculptors; and the large **Godt-Cleary Arts 5** (1217 South Main Street; tel: 702-452-2000; www.gcarts-lv.com; Tue–Sat 10am–6pm) exhibits works by big-name New York artists, both past and contemporary.

Not too far away, and worth a look if you are keen on art by living artists, is the **Contemporary Arts Collective 6** (231 West Charleston Boulevard; tel: 702-382-3886; www.lasvegascac. org). One of Las Vegas's oldest galleries, it is a non-profit-making co-operative, showcasing contemporary sculpture, painting, and mixed-media work by many of the city's top artists. Once part of the Arts Factory, the collective recently moved to the ground floor of the new Holsum Lofts, an historic building that was originally a bread factory.

At this point, we suggest returning to your hotel or the Strip by retracing the route to cool off, rest up, and get dressed for dinner.

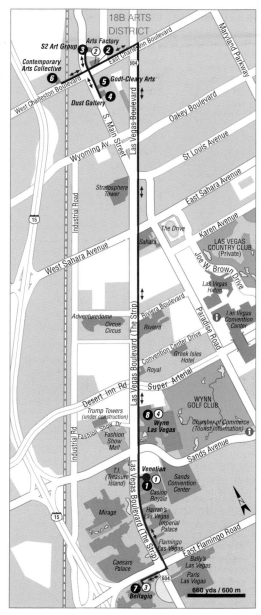

BELLAGIO GALLERY

Classical Concerts

The Las Vegas Philharmonic presents classical music concerts once a month from October through May, on Sat evenings at the University of Nevada – Las Vegas Concert Hall. For schedule and tickets, call 702-258-5438 or visit www.lasvegas philharmonic.com.

Whenever the subject of art in Las Vegas comes up, somebody is sure to mention the **Bellagio** ❼ (3595 Las Vegas Boulevard South; tel: 702-693-7871; www.bellagioresort.com; *see also pp.45 and 112*), about three blocks south of the Venetian and across the street. Former owner Steve Wynn took most of his art collection along when he sold the Bellagio, and today the hotel's **Bellagio Gallery of Fine Art** (Sun–Thur 10am–6pm, Fri–Sat 10am–9pm; charge) displays temporary exhibits that are curated by major Southwestern universities.

Recent shows have included photography by Ansel Adams and ceramics by Pablo Picasso. Call the hotel or visit the website for details of the current show. Even if it does not appeal, a visit to the Bellagio is certainly worthwhile, if only to see *Fiori di Como*, the spectacular 2,000-sq-ft (186-sq m) field of colorful blown glass flowers that is American glass artist Dale Chihuly's crowning achievement, and which covers the lobby ceiling.

EVENING OPTIONS

Ideas for dinner include staying at the Bellagio for a meal at the **Picasso**, see 🍴③, if you have reservations, or heading down the Strip to Wynn Las Vegas *(see below)*, for a less formal meal at **Wynn Buffet,** see 🍴④, and – if you are in the mood for further activities and culture – art and a show at the Wynn Las Vegas hotel.

WYNN LAS VEGAS

For the latter option, taxi down the Strip to the towering **Wynn Las Vegas** ❽ (3131 Las Vegas Boulevard South; tel: 701-693-7871; www.wynnlas vegas.com; *see also pp.62 and 111*), home to Steve Wynn's art collection. After the sale of the Bellagio, Wynn eventually moved the bulk of the paintings he had originally exhibited there to his new hotel, where he tried to charge an even steeper entrance fee. Because of sluggish ticket sales, he closed the exhibit in

---

Food and Drink

③ PICASSO

Bellagio Hotel, 3595 Las Vegas Boulevard South; tel: 702-693-7223; Wed–Mon 6–9:30pm; $$$$

This elegant French-Mediterranean restaurant, designed as a tribute to Pablo Picasso by his son Claude, is decorated with original Picasso paintings valued at $50 million, making the $100-plus price of a four-course prix-fixe meal or a five-course chef's dégustation menu seem like a bargain. (Just remember that many Las Vegas visitors lose far greater sums at the casino tables in less time than it takes to dine here.) Menus change seasonally. A typical meal might include poached oysters garnished with caviar; shrimp with roasted pears; breast of pheasant with morel mushrooms; and the dessert of the day. A bonus is the fabulous view of the lake in front of the hotel, where hundreds of fountains dance to music every half-hour during the afternoon and every 15 minutes after dark.

④ WYNN BUFFET

Wynn Las Vegas, 3131 Las Vegas Boulevard South; tel: 702-770-3340; Mon–Fri 8–10:30am, 11am–3:30pm, 4–10pm, Sat–Sun 8:30am–3:30pm, 4–10pm; $$–$$$

Another good bet – and somewhat more affordable than the Picasso – is the chic buffet at the Wynn Las Vegas. Filled with flowers and white wicker, the decor alone is enough to set this dining room apart from other gourmet all-you-can-eateries on the Strip. The amazing array of foods includes 17 active cooking stations offering everything from thick steaks to sushi and Alaskan king crab legs to down-home country-fried chicken.

2006 and hung many of the paintings, including works by Turner, Van Gogh, Vermeer, Gaugin, Matisse and Warhol, around the common areas of the hotel, where you gaze upon them while you wait for *Le Rêve (see below)* to start.

Le Rêve

A blatant attempt to beat the Cirque du Soleil company *(see pp.55 and 71)* at its own game, *Le Rêve* (French for "The Dream") was conceived by Cirque's former creative director, Franco Dragone. Using multi-level pools of water instead of a stage, the theater-in-the-round production (tel: 702-770-7100; show starts at 10:30pm) features acrobatics, swimmers, live music and birds, and special effects (such as rain, snow, and fire), and mesmerizes audiences with scenes that are by turns whimsical, surreal, and nightmarish.

Above from far left: Bellagio and fountains; detail of Dale Chihuly's spectacular glass, in the Bellagio; Steve Wynn and *(right)* his vast Wynn Las Vegas.

Steve Wynn's Picasso

The show *Le Rêve (pictured below)* was named after Wynn's favorite Picasso painting, a blue-period portrait of the painter's 21-year-old mistress, Marie-Thérèse Walter. Wynn had also originally planned to use the title as the name for his new hotel. He had bought the Picasso in 1997 for a whopping $48.4 million. Nine years later, a Las Vegas legend started when he agreed to sell it to another collector for $139 million – the highest price ever paid for a painting. The story goes that a day after Wynn signed the contract, but before the sale was completed, he was showing the painting to guests, including television journalist Barbara Walters and screenwriter Nora Ephron, at a cocktail party in his penthouse. Wynn, who claims to lack peripheral vision because of a medical condition, gestured at the painting – and poked a 6-in (15-cm) tear in it with his elbow. Wynn's comment, according to Ephron, was "Oh, shit, look what I've done. Thank God it was me." Lloyds of London, insurer of the painting, settled with Wynn for an undisclosed amount in April 2007, and he has since announced that he does intend to get the painting restored.

INTERNATIONAL VEGAS

Built in 1966, Caesars Palace was the first of the city's themed casinos that married American-style glitz and excess with international cultural references. After Vegas's fortunes dwindled in the 1980s, a new breed of casino emerged, heralding the age of the megaresort.

Above: international scenes: the Statue of Liberty at New York New York; German character at the Hofbräuhaus; Eiffel Tower at Paris Las Vegas.

Above from left: exterior of Paris Las Vegas; spectacular glass inside the hotel's dome.

DISTANCE 4 miles (7km), plus an optional 2-mile (3-km) detour for lunch)

TIME Around 5½ hours, not including lunch

START Paris Las Vegas Hotel

END Mandalay Bay (or Paris Las Vegas, if you end with the suggested show)

POINTS TO NOTE

The tour is done on foot or monorail, with a taxi necessary for the lunch option. If you do want to see *Spamalot* (the recommended show), ensure you book well in advance (see pp.47 and 105 for details); it is advisable also to make a dinner reservation for Okada.

Food and Drink 🍴

① LE VILLAGE BUFFET

Paris Las Vegas Hotel, 3655 Las Vegas Boulevard South; tel: 702-967-4859; daily 7am–10pm; $$
Unlike other hotels' broadly international buffets, this one is unusual in that the food is almost all French. Fill up on crêpes, pastries, sausages, cheeses, fruit, and much more. Delicious coffee, too. Savor it all in various dining settings that reflect different kinds of French provincial architecture.

In the 1980s, Las Vegas's economic and population growth rates slumped to one-sixth of what it had been during the 1950s and '60s. Part of the reason may have been that organized crime funding dried up, but the biggest factors were probably the legalization of gambling in Atlantic City, New Jersey in 1976 and federal court rulings that opened the door to Native American casinos in 1979. Gambling was no longer enough to draw tourists to this isolated desert outpost. Opportunity awaited the developer who could figure out how to keep the town from drying up and blowing away.

That developer was Steve Wynn, who parlayed his part-ownership in a downtown casino as well as using his contacts with billionaire Howard Hughes and junk-bond magnate Michael Milliken into a deal to build the world's most expensive hotel. That hotel was the Mirage, the prototype for the huge megaresorts that fill the southern Strip today.

International Theme Park

Improbable as it seemed, the "If you build it, they will come" approach worked so well that within a decade, more than a dozen of the world's largest destination hotels had sprung

up along a mile (2km) of Las Vegas Boulevard South, distinguished from one another by themes that paid tribute to various nations of the world. Together, they formed a single international theme park, much like Disney's Epcot Center in Orlando but on a grand scale. Today, the most popular pastime for Las Vegas visitors is wandering this section of the Strip to "see the world" in a day.

PARIS LAS VEGAS

Since the lunch recommendation on this itinerary is off-Strip, non-drivers may wish to simplify their day by filling up at the all-you-can-eat breakfast buffet at **Le Village Buffet**, see ⑪①, at **Paris Las Vegas** ❶ (3655 Las Vegas Boulevard South; tel: 702-946-7000 or 888-266-5687; www.parislas vegas.com; *see p.115*) and then just choosing another lunch stop. (On the Strip, you are never more than about 100ft (30m) from food, so there are plenty of options and alternatives.)

GLOBAL VIEW

South of Paris Las Vegas, most of the themed hotels are on the west side of the street, and you can get a helpful overview by walking along the east side first to see them from a distance. Head down past **Bally's** *(see p.111)*, **Bill's**, the **Flamingo** *(see pp.30, 34, and 112)*, Jimmy Buffet's Margaritaville eatery and the Harley-Davidson Café, and you'll also pass the **Imperial Palace** ❷ (3535 Las Vegas Boulevard South; tel:

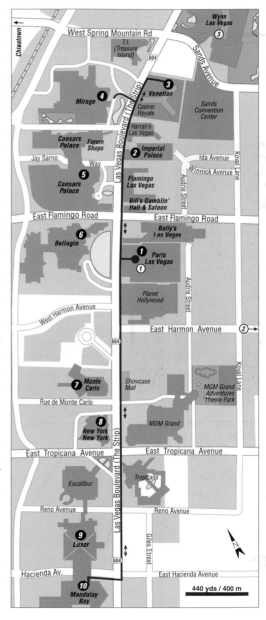

Above: cocktails at Bellagio.

Previous Life
The Venetian now occupies the site of the famous Sands hotel that closed its doors in 1996. Among the stars who played the Sands' Copa Room were Frank Sinatra (who also co-owned the hotel at that time), Dean Martin, and Sammy Davis Jr., key players among the so-called "Rat Pack" group of entertainers, who were emblems of what many consider to be the golden age of Vegas *(see p.31)*.

Right: part of the inside of the Venetian replicates the Paris opera house. More authentically Italian are the thousands of pigeons that fly out of the hotel at least twice a day.

702-731-3311), an older, low-priced hotel that, despite its Asian rooflines and Chinese dragon motifs, is not in nearly the same league as the modern themed megaresorts nearby. Although negotiating the front entrance clogged with taxis and hucksters is rather stressful, you may consider it if you want to visit the hotel's large first-rate **automobile collection** (daily 9:30am–9:30pm, free).

THE VENETIAN

Now continue along the Strip to the breathtaking **Venetian ③** (3355 Las Vegas Boulevard South; tel: 702-414-1000; www.venetian.com; *see pp.36 and 50, and 111)*. It is a reigning monarch among the Vegas destination resorts, where the two main attractions are the

Guggenheim-Hermitage Museum *(see p.37)* and the **Grand Canal Shoppes** (Sun–Thur 10am–11pm, Fri–Sat 10am–midnight). The latter is one of the most impressive of the international hotels' malls, with its gondolas, *trompe l'oeil* and floodlit sky, street performers, living statues, all set in a grand-scale replica of St. Mark's Square in Venice.

THE MIRAGE

Cross the Strip to the tropical-themed **Mirage ④** (3400 Las Vegas Boulevard South; tel: 702-791-7111; www. mirage.com; *see pp.32 and 110)*, the megaresort that started it all. When the Mirage first opened, it drew huge crowds of curious spectators right from the beginning. Within three years, the casino was the biggest money-maker on the Strip. Even though the hotel needed to take more than a million dollars a day to break even, it never seemed to be a problem. Today, the crowds still come for the lush rain-forest entrance, tropical ambience, and white tigers – not to mention the vol-cano in front of the hotel. Its shopping mall, the Street of Shops, is designed to resemble an exclusive European shopping boulevard.

CAESARS PALACE

Two blocks south is the Ancient Rome-themed **Caesars Palace ⑤** (3570 Las Vegas Boulevard South, tel: 702-731-7110; *see pp.62, 78, and 112)*, which reigned as the city's most opulent resort

from the time its doors opened in 1966 until the completion of the Mirage 23 years later. It has kept pace over the years, expanding to five times its original size, and remains one of the Strip's most impressive megaresorts.

Forum Shops

Giant Roman columns, mosaic floor patterns, and outsized reproductions of Classical Roman sculptures make exploring this resort fun. In particular, check out the **Forum Shops** (Sun–Thur 10am–11pm, Fri–Sat 10am–midnight), a labyrinth of upscale designer boutiques that is among the most exclusive shopping zones in the US.

BELLAGIO

Continue another block south to the **Bellagio ❻** (3600 Las Vegas Boulevard South; tel: 702-731-7110; www.bellagioresort.com; *see pp.40 and 112*), styled after the town of the same name on Lake Como, Italy. The hotel's best-known attractions include its **Gallery of Fine Art** *(see p.40)* and the spectacular **fountain show** performed in the "lake" in front of the hotel at frequent intervals from mid-afternoon until midnight. Especially worth a visit is the Conservatory and Botanical Gardens (24hr; free) just off the main lobby, where exotic plants and flowers create a riot of color, fragrance, and shape.

MONTE CARLO

Two more blocks south, on the same side of the road, is the more afford-ably priced sister hotel to the Bellagio, the **Monte Carlo ❼** (3770 Las Vegas Boulevard South; tel: 702-730-7777; www.monte-carlo.com; *see p.114*). The two are usually connected by a tram, but it is advisable to call beforehand to check the link is working. Although the Monte Carlo has no real sightseeing attractions of its own, the casino is worth a peek because of its lavish decor, which is inspired by the place du Casino in Monte Carlo, Monaco. The hotel is a convenient place to catch a taxi if you're going out to the Ger-

Above from far left: gondolier at the Venetian; Caesar at his palace.

Did You Know?
The Dunes, located where the Bellagio stands today, presented the first topless showgirls in 1957.

Chinatown

The American Southwest has had a sizeable Chinese population ever since laborers were imported to build railroads in the late 19th century. However, Las Vegas has only had a well-defined Chinatown since 1995, when a Taiwanese developer built Chinatown Plaza (Spring Mountain Road at Valley View Boulevard) and enticed many Asians to move to Las Vegas and open businesses here. Today, three other major Asian shopping centers have opened in the same area and Chinese residents are the fastest-growing ethnic group in Las Vegas today, accounting for about five percent of the population. Filipino, Vietnamese, Japanese and Korean communities also reside in the Chinatown area.

Above from left: the Mandalay Bay, with the monorail out front; replica of the tomb of Egyptian Pharoah Tutankhamun at the Luxor.

Above: the unmistakable Lady Liberty at New York New York.

manic **Hofbräuhaus**, see ⑪②, for lunch. (If you are driving, head up either East Harmon Avenue or East Tropicana Avenue, both of which intersect with Paradise Road.)

NEW YORK NEW YORK

Back on the Strip, continue your tour at **New York New York** ❽ (3790 Las Vegas Boulevard South; tel: 702-740-6969; www.nynyhotelcasino.com; *see pp.88 and 115)*, an amazing homage to the Big Apple, with residential towers designed to look like skyscrapers and a

casino styled after Central Park, complete with trees. You'll also find replicas of the Statue of Liberty and Brooklyn Bridge, and a Coney Island-style amusement center, complete with a roller-coaster.

LUXOR

Next stop, another couple of blocks south and past the Disney-castle-style Excalibur *(see pp.51 and 112)*, still on the same side of the Strip, is the shining black pyramidal **Luxor** ❾ (3900 Las Vegas Boulevard South; tel: 702-262-4000; www.luxor.com; *see p.113)*. One level up from the casino floor, you enter the world's largest atrium, with 29 million sq ft (3 million sq m) containing all of the resort's restaurants, shops, and theaters.

One of the Luxor's attractions is the **King Tut Museum** (daily 10am–11pm; charge). This precise replica of the tomb of Egyptian Pharoah Tutankhamun was created from the notes of British archaeologist Howard Carter, who discovered the actual tomb in 1922. The museum contains replicas of the gold sarcophagus, chariot, guardian statues, and hundreds of other objects found in the tomb, all reproduced by hand using the same tools and 3,300-year-old techniques. The 15 minutes visitors are allowed to view the exhibit is not nearly enough time.

MANDALAY BAY

Next door, the large, showy, gold-hued **Mandalay Bay** ❿ (3950 Las Vegas

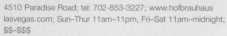

Food and Drink

② HOFBRÄUHAUS

4510 Paradise Road; tel: 702-853-3227; www.hofbrauhaus lasvegas.com; Sun–Thur 11am–11pm, Fri–Sat 11am–midnight; $$–$$$

Located one mile (2km) east of the Strip, the Hofbräuhaus is the city's only major German-themed establishment. This vast restaurant and beer garden, with its 45ft-high (14m) muraled ceiling, is a lookalike franchise owned by the 400-year-old brewery of the same name founded by the Duke of Bavaria in Munich, Germany. It features imported Hofbrauhaus beer, an Oktoberfest atmosphere, and authentic German foods like *Sauerbraten,* a Bavarian pot roast, and *Riesen Fleischpflanzerl*, a sort of pork-and-beef hamburger.

③ OKADA

Wynn Las Vegas, 3131 Las Vegas Boulevard South; tel: 702-248-3463; Sun–Thur 5:30–10:30pm, Fri–Sat 5:30–11:30pm; $$–$$$$

While Las Vegas has a myriad Japanese restaurants, few can hold a candle to the one at the Wynn. Set beside the hotel's waterfall and lagoon, and designed with plenty of glass and wood, stone pathways, and greenery, the restaurant features an outstanding sushi bar, a long menu of dishes cooked *tepanyaki*-style (stir-fried on a hot tabletop) or *robata*-style (grilled over open flames), along with a wide selection of sakes. A typical entrée is braised *kurobuta* short rib with fingerling potatoes, *cippolini* onion, *shishito* pepper, and ginger-soy caramel broth. For a real splurge, try the Kobe beef sirloin.

Boulevard South, tel: 702-632-777; www.mandalaybay. com; *see pp.35, 70 and 114)* has a nebulous Southeast Asian concept apparently inspired by Rudyard Kipling's poem *Mandalay*, though there is no bay anywhere near the actual landlocked town of Mandalay, Myanmar (formerly Burma).

No matter. The Mandalay Bay's real theme seems to be an imaginary tropical paradise, replete with artificial foliage and waterfalls as well as strange statues of fantastical creatures such as earless unicorns and musical frogs. Asian visitors note the resemblance to new casinos in Macau, the semi-autonomous administrative region of China where several Las Vegas gaming corporations – including the Mandalay Bay's parent company, MGM Mirage – are building lavish new resorts. Look out for the Eye Candy bar, with its cool bright lights.

DINNER

To continue the international theme at the end of the tour, a good choice for dinner would be the Japanese **Okada**, see ⑪③, at Wynn Las Vegas *(see pp.40, 62, and 111)*. The hotel is at the northern end of the Strip, so possibly best reached by taxi, if your energy is starting to flag.

MONTY PYTHON'S SPAMALOT

Representing the United Kingdom on our international odyssey is our suggestion for the evening's entertainment.

This wacky and irreverant musical comedy, written by former Monty Python member Eric Idle and directed by Mike Nichols, is loosely based on the 1975 film *Monty Python and the Holy Grail*. The stage version of the film was a hit on Broadway and in London; its Las Vegas version (performed at Wynn Las Vegas; tel: 702-770-9966; shows: Sun, Mon, Wed 8pm; Tue, Fri, Sat 10pm) is spiced up with showgirls and plenty of in-jokes and catchy phrases.

Pyramidal Design
The rooms in the Luxor's huge pyramid have one sloping glass wall overlooking the main floor.

Below: Las Vegas is a great place to try cuisine of all nationalities, including Japanese sushi.

LAS VEGAS WITH KIDS

While Sin City is no longer branding itself as a family-friendly destination, it does have diversions that are suitable for children. Teenagers might find suitable attractions a little thin on the ground though...

Toys of Yesteryear
A toy store where adults have more fun than kids, Toys of Yesteryear (2028 East Charleston Boulevard; tel: 702-598-4030) is a unique antique store packed with toys from the mid-20th century. Digging through the constantly changing stock, you may find yourself swept away by nostalgia at the sight of vintage Barbie dolls, stuffed animals, classic board games, electric trains, and miniature racing cars.

Above from left: merry-go-round in the Adventuredome; dolls come too; the kids having fun; neon at Circus Circus.

DISTANCE 4 miles (6km) for the afternoon tour plus 2 miles (3km) for the dinner show
TIME Around 6 hours (tour only)
START/END Circus Circus
POINTS TO NOTE
For this route, take the bus (CAT route 108; free for five year olds and under), a taxi or drive. Reservations are recommended at the Quark Bar & Restaurant. Buy tickets up to 60 days in advance for the *Tournament of Kings* show.

For a few years in the 1990s, Vegas tried to promote itself as a family destination. Though it never amounted to serious competition for Orlando in Florida, it did draw a lot of parents with kids in tow, and often acted as a gateway for trips to the Grand Canyon and other Southwestern vacation meccas.

There was just one problem. By law, children aren't allowed to gamble: casinos rake in a lot more money than roller-coasters, so image shapers did an abrupt U-turn to revive the old Sin City image with their now-familiar "What happens in Vegas..." pitch. Still, kids love the lights and over-the-top spectacle, and the amusement rides on offer just keep getting better and better.

CIRCUS CIRCUS

Start the day with breakfast at the child-friendly **Circus Circus ❶** (2880 Las Vegas Boulevard South; tel: 702-734-0410 or 800-444-2472; www.circuscircus.com; *see p.110*), at the Circus Buffet, see ⍟①.

Adventuredome

At around 10am, head for Circus Circus's **Adventuredome** (summer: daily 10am–midnight, call or visit website for opening times for the rest of the year; charge). This domed complex is said to be America's largest indoor amusement park, though its 5 acres (2 hectares) doesn't seem as big as it sounds like it should be, and the rides slot together like puzzle pieces to make the most of the space. They include thrill rides such as the Canyon Blaster – a double loop, double corkscrew roller-coaster (riders must be at least 4ft or 122cm tall) – and the soaking-wet Rim Runner, which plunges you down a 60-ft (18-m) waterfall. There are also bumper cars, a swinging pirate ship, and tame junior rides to keep the little ones happy.

Circus Acts and Midway

Also at Circus Circus are performances by trapeze artists, tightrope walkers

and other daredevils (daily 11am–midnight; free); extraordinarily, these take place at regular intervals high above the casino floor, with a safety net to protect the slot machine players from falling performers. The best vantage point for watching both the circus acts and the gamblers is from the mezzanine, much of which serves as a carnival-style midway with ball-throwing games and other feats of skill you can play to win stuffed toys and similar prizes. The midway also has a number of child-oriented shops such as Nothing But Clowns, Sweet Tooth, and Circus Kids.

LUNCH

At around 12:30pm, it is time to move on from Circus Circus by walking along Riviera Boulevard to cross the Strip. Keep on walking (if it is just too hot, or the kids are too hungry, hop in a cab) for one block, until you reach

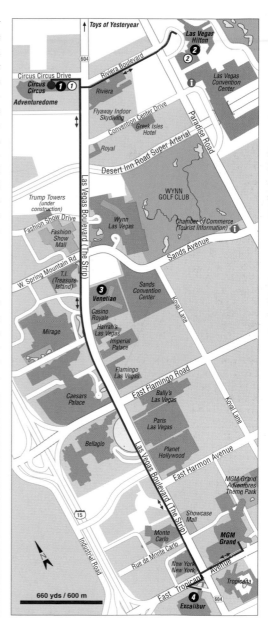

Above: figures from *Star Trek*.

Hotel Options
Both Circus Circus and Excalibur are excellent choices if you are visiting Las Vegas with children. Little ones stay for free at Circus Circus when accompanied by their parents, while children under the age of 12 stay for free at Excalibur. Needless to say, those who aren't visiting with kids may prefer to stay somewhere else, where the average age per guest is rather higher!

the **Las Vegas Hilton** ❷ (3000 Paradise Road; tel: 702-697-8700; www. lv-hilton.com), home to **Quark's Bar and Restaurant**, see ⑪②, which is our recommendation for lunch and is located within our next suggested family attraction.

Alternatively, you can continue up the strip (catch the CAT route 108) to the MGM **Grand** (3799 Las Vegas Boulevard South, tel: 702-891-1111; www.mgmgrand.com; *see also pp.35 and 114*), and then have lunch at the hotel's **Rainforest Café** *(see p.35)* if you prefer a more natural kind of theme. It is a bit of a detour, so if you do decide to go to the MGM Grand for lunch, why not visit the MGM **Lion Habitat** *(see p.35)* while you are there.

> ## Food and Drink 🍴
> ### ② QUARK'S BAR & RESTAURANT
> Las Vegas Hilton, 3000 Paradise Road; tel: 702-697-8725; Sun–Thur 11:30am–10pm, Fri–Sat 11:30am–11pm; $–$$
> Die-hard Trekkies and kids alike love this place where uniformed servers take your order on tricorders and Klingons and Ferengi might stroll over to your table to help you pick your way through the 24th-century menu. Try Flaming Ribs of Targ (a huge rack of pesto-covered pork ribs that are ignited at your table), chicken wings in a Vulcan hot sauce, or Klingon Kabob. Portions are generous and the food is rated higher than that at most other Vegas themed joints by diners. Adults might want to sneak off to the adjacent bar for a bright blue Romulan Ale or a cocktail such as the Harry Mudd martini.

STAR TREK EXPERIENCE

The Las Vegas Hilton's **Star Trek – The Experience** (www.startrekexp. com; daily 11:30am–8:30pm; charge) is part museum, part show, and part ride. It is also budget-busting. Expect to come face to face with (not-so-hostile aliens, the crew of the *Starship Enterprise* – in fact, the heroes of all the *Star Trek* series. Adults may have to explain to kids exactly who Captain Kirk and Mr. Spock were, but no matter. The 3D (and "4D") special effects in the Borg Invasion are incredibly realistic, as are the live "alien" actors, while the Klingon Encounter involves a high-speed chase through space to escape enemy warships. The museum has the world's largest collection of *Star Trek* memorabilia.

WAXWORKS

In the mid-afternoon, head back to the Strip along Riviera Boulevard, and bus down it to the **Venetian** ❸ (3377 Las Vegas Boulevard South; tel: 702-862-7800; www.venetian.com; *see pp.36 and 111*) for **Madame Tussaud's Interactive Attraction** (daily 10am–10pm; charge). This pricy museum contains more than 300 life-size, uncannily realistic wax figures of celebrities and historical figures from George Washington and Abraham Lincoln to the Dalai Lama, Julia Roberts, and Britney Spears. It's "interactive" because you are invited not only to touch the figures but also have your photograph taken posing in bunny ears with Hugh Hefner, mar-

rying George Clooney, singing along with Elvis Presley or playing golf with Tiger Woods. It's educational, too – after a certain fashion.

Alternatively, or in addition to the waxworks, you may want to see if you can take a **gondola ride** (Sun–Thur 10am–11pm, Fri–Sat 10am–midnight; charge) along the hotel's "Grand Canal." Reservations must be made in person, on the same day only.

EVENING OPTIONS

At this point, there are two options, both intended to tie in with a dinner show at **Excalibur ❹** (3850 Las Vegas Boulevard South; tel: 702-597-7600; shows Wed–Mon 6pm, 8:30pm; charge; *see p.112*), which is back up the Strip (just past the MGM Grand). There are two showings a night (except Tue), so, depending on whether you want to go for the early or late one, you can either head directly there or you can fit in a short rest at your hotel beforehand.

Tournament of Kings

Our suggested show for the evening is Excalibur's *Tournament of Kings*. This 75-minute dinner extravaganza features nonstop action, with jousting knights, swordfights, horse races, pyrotechnics, and general uproar, as audiences cheer their combatants on, based on which area of the hall they are sitting in.

The medieval theme carries over to the tasty banquet fare, served just before the show starts. Starting with "dragon's blood" (tomato soup), you also get a

whole roast Cornish game hen with potato, vegetables, non-alcoholic beverages, and dessert. But you don't get silverware. In true Dark Ages fashion, you dine with your fingers.

Magicians

Las Vegas has even more magicians than Elvis impersonators. A family favorite (and easy on the wallet) is Mac King, who performs afternoon shows at Harrah's (3475 Las Vegas Boulevard South; tel: 702-785-5555; Tue–Sat 1pm, 2pm, 3pm, 4pm; charge). Quirky and comical, King is best known for his Amazing Goldfish Trick, catching live fish over the heads of the audience on a fishing line baited with Fig Newtons. Other magicians include Lance Burton, a permanent headliner at the Monte Carlo (3770 Las Vegas Boulevard South; tel: 702-730-7777; shows Tue and Sat 7pm and 10pm, Wed–Fri 7pm only). Burton, one of the world's leading "classical" magicians, specializes in venerable illusions such as white doves out of nowhere, vanishings and reappearances, and levitations in a theater built especially for him. Part of the proceeds from his kid-friendly shows and magic shop are donated to charities for mentally and physically challenged children. Some of the less traditional Las Vegas magic acts are less suitable for children: Penn and Teller's show is billed as family-friendly, though moms of younger kids may not appreciate the spurting blood illusions, and don't take kids to see shock magician the Amazing Jonathan's raunchy show.

THRILL-SEEKERS' LAS VEGAS

It used to be that the casino floor provided all the excitement a visitor to Vegas could want. But now speed, heights, and adventures in Cyberspace also make the heart beat faster – and prices will take your breath away, too.

Above from left:
rides for dare-devils; Stratosphere Tower; test your driving capabilities at the NASCAR Café; vertiginous views on the Stratosphere Tower's X Scream ride.

Skydiving For Real
If you want the Real McCoy, make arrangements through Skydive Las Vegas (tel: 702-759-3483; www.skydive lasvegas.com), Las Vegas Skydiving Center (tel: 866-688-2378; www.lasvegas skydivingcenter.com); or Las Vegas Extreme Skydiving (tel: 866-398-5867; www. vegasextremesky diving.com). All offer beginners' lessons, tandem freefalls (where an instructor holds you), and even skydiving weddings.

DISTANCE 1.5 miles (2km) round trip plus optional monorail ride
TIME A full day
START The Sahara
END Stratosphere Tower
POINTS TO NOTE
Buy an all-day pass for the monorail. There's also an all-day pass for the Sahara's rides. Reservations are strongly advised for *Diego*. Reserve well ahead for MGM Grand's *Kà*.

Gambling has always been an effective way for Las Vegas visitors to get their adrenalin racing. But today, the Strip offers many other state-of-the-art experiences that rival the top rides in any of the world's best amusement parks (and some cost more, too). Even jaded vacationers who find slot machines and roulette kind of boring will get their fill of sudden rushes in this itinerary and be ready by the end of the day to head for the casino just to relax and take it easy. By the way, do not drink until dinner: tickets for most of the activities on this itinerary won't be sold to you if alcohol can be detected on your breath or drugs in your demeanor.

INDOOR SKYDIVING

Let your breakfast digest properly before you start with some indoor skydiving at **Flyaway Indoor Skydiving** ❶ (200 Convention Center Drive; tel: 702-731-4768 or 877-545-8093; www. flyawayindoorskydiving.com; daily 10am–7pm; charge; note: under 18s must be accompanied by adult; no sandals or open-toed shoes are allowed, and no persons the management considers obese will be permitted to ride).

The Experience
If you've never tried skydiving before, this is an uncannily realistic way to simulate the experience. If you have, this three-minute ride lasts longer than the real thing usually does. You are given 20 minutes of live and video instruction on how to fly and land, then a DC-3 propeller blasts you up into a 22-ft (7-m) vertical wind tunnel, simulating a 120-mph (190-kph) free fall. Unlike actual skydiving, though, you don't have to worry about whether your parachute will open – because you're not wearing one. Expensive, true, but this really is a once-in-a-lifetime opportunity to experience flying, Superman-style.

STRATOSPHERE TOWER

The only thing missing from Flyaway is the view of the ground rushing up at you from far below. For that, take a short cab or bus ride down to the north end of the Strip and the **Stratosphere Tower ❷** (2000 Las Vegas Boulevard South; tel: 702-380-7777; Sun–Thur 10am–1am, Fri-Sat 10am– 2am; separate charge for admission and for individual rides; riders must be at least 4ft 6in/137cm tall). Without a doubt, this is where you'll find the most shocking thrill rides on the Strip.

The observation tower near the top of the tallest structure in Las Vegas (1,149ft, 350m) commands a jaw-dropping 360-degree view of the city and the surrounding mountains and desert, and the high-speed glass elevator up to the indoor and outdoor observation decks is a thrill in itself.

Three Rides

The three rides off the observation decks are the highest (above ground level) amusement park-style rides in the world. The **Big Shot** shoots you up a 160-ft (49-m) tower in 2.5 seconds, then drops you back down weightlessly to bungee up and down until you land. Or there's **Insanity**, which seats you at the end of a 64-ft (19-m) arm that spins you outward at an angle of 70 degrees with nothing between you and the Strip nearly 100 stories below. The scariest of the three rides, though, is **X Scream**. You enter an eight-pas-senger car that hoists you to the top of a 27-ft (8-m) arm and then the car

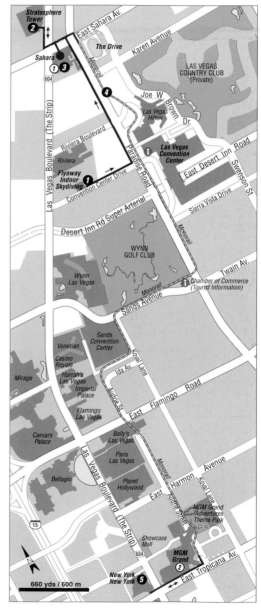

Helicopter Tours

Due to safety issues, the exciting Grand Canyon tours offered from Vegas do not fly into the canyon, but stay at rim level, offering incomparable views. Tour companies include Heli USA Flights (tel: 702-736-8787 or 800-359-8727, www.heliusa.com); Maverick Helicopters (tel: 702-261-0007 or 888-261-4414, www.maverickhelicopter.com); Papillon Grand Canyon Helicopters (tel: 736-7243 or 888-635-7272, www.papillon.com); and Sundance Helicopters (tel: 736-0606, www.helicoptour.com).

drops you over the edge of the deck and downward, jerking to a sudden stop in midair. The experience is sure to bring alive your most basic nightmare of falling.

SAHARA

The next stop is the **Sahara** ❸ (2535 Las Vegas Boulevard South; tel: 702-737-2111 or 888-696-2121; www.saharavegas.com; *see p.110*), where for thrills at the wheel, enter the NASCAR **Cafe Entertainment Center** (located within the Sahara), home to the state-of-the-art Pit Pass Video Arcade and a couple of breathtaking rides.

Las Vegas Cyber Speedway

The first is **Las Vegas Cyber Speedway** (Sun–Thur 11am–8pm, Fri–Sat 11am–10pm; charge). Here, you can "drive" up

to 220 miles per hour (354kph) in authentic stock car and Indy car racing simulators, mounted in front of wraparound screens that display your choice of the Las Vegas Motor Speedway or the Las Vegas Strip. Stick shift or automatic transmission cars are available. Engine and environment sounds roar through a 15-speaker sound system, and the hydraulics deliver a totally convincing illusion of speed and centrifugal force. Bumps and crashes are startlingly realistic, too. It's first-come, first-served, except for groups (you can reserve up to eight cars to race each other), so expect a wait. The ride lasts 8 minutes.

Speed: the Ride

Next is **Speed: The Ride** (adjacent to the NASCAR Café; Sun–Thur 11am–8pm, Fri–Sat 11am–10pm; charge). Of the several roller-coasters on the Strip, we've chosen to recommend this one for its convenient location and unique configuration. It goes out a tunnel beside the NASCAR Café, then under the sidewalk, through the neon Sahara sign and up a 250-ft (76-m) tower. Then, after a giddy, seemingly endless moment of weightlessness, it plunges backward all the way to its starting point.

Before you leave the Sahara – and, more importantly, if you can stomach food at this point – a good option for lunch is the NASCAR **Café**, see ⑪①.

MONORAIL

After lunch, it's time for a trip on the **Las Vegas monorail** ❹ (tel: 702-699-7200; Mon–Thur 7am–2am, Fri–Sun

---

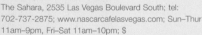

Food and Drink

① NASCAR CAFÉ

The Sahara, 2535 Las Vegas Boulevard South; tel: 702-737-2875; www.nascarcafelasvegas.com; Sun–Thur 11am–9pm, Fri–Sat 11am–10pm; $

This appropriately noisy speedway motif eatery serves a large selection of rib-sticking American food, including six different kinds of burgers, chicken-fried steak, and baby back ribs. There's also the Brickyard Platter, a pile of Buffalo wings, spring rolls, mozzarella sticks, and onion wings with assorted dipping sauces. You can watch others drive the Cyber Speedway and ride "Speed: The Ride" while you dine.

② EMERIL'S NEW ORLEANS FISH HOUSE

MGM Grand, 3799 Las Vegas Boulevard South; tel: 702-891-7374; www.emerils.com; daily 5:30–10:30pm; $$$

Whether it is scallops from Maine, pike from the Midwest, or redfish from Texas, celebrity chef Emeril Lagasse "kicks it up a notch" with Creole-Cajun flair in a setting that is more Bourbon Street than the Strip. Especially tasty is the house specialty, New Orleans barbeque shrimp. Meat and chicken dishes also available.

7am–3am; charge), which you board outside the hotel. The ride south to the end of the line takes you past all the hotels on the east side of the Strip, offering a quick tour of such megaresorts as the Venetian *(see pp.36, 50, and 111)*, Paris Las Vegas *(see pp.43 and 115)* and, at the end, the MGM Grand *(see pp.35, 50, and 115)*, from two stories above sidewalk level. The trip takes around 30 minutes return.

MANHATTAN EXPRESS

At the MGM Grand hop off the monorail and walk west along Tropicana Avenue to cross the Strip and reach **New York New York ⑤** *(see pp.46, 89, and 115)*. (The façade – a copy of the New York skyline – is impossible to miss.) Outside, the **Manhattan Express** (Sun–Thur 11am–11pm, Fri–Sat 10.30am–midnight; charge) is the original Strip resort roller-coaster; it careers at speeds up to 67mph (108kph) along the hotel roofline and above replicas of skyscrapers, New York Harbor, and the Statue of Liberty. The 3-minute ride features two drops of more than 100ft (30m), a unique 180-degree heartline twist and dive, and a 540-degree spiral.

EVENING SUGGESTIONS

One option for the evening is a night at the MGM **Grand**, where you can have dinner at **Emeril's New Orleans Fish House**, ①② and then catch the show by **Cirque du Soleil** (tel: 702-531-3000 or 866-774-7117; Tue–Sat 7pm and 9:30pm), which makes for a suitably

breathtaking end to this thrill-seeking day. In the show, entitled 'Kà', the action is played out on a five-story-tall stage with a floor that raises from horizontal to vertical in mid-performance. Barbarian pirates swing across the theater on ropes and shoot flaming arrows over the heads of the audience. Sinking ships, young lovers, bursts of fireworks, strange languages, swordfights, and, of course, the most unbelievable acrobatics add up to an unforgettable entertainment experience.

Above from far left: two scenes at the NASCAR Café Entertainment Center.

Below: the thrilling *Kà*.

LADIES-ONLY VEGAS

One result of the city cleaning up its act is that there are now more female visitors than male ones. So, join the crowd and leave the men behind for a day of pampering, retail therapy, and some kicked-back fun with the girls.

Lovely Spas

Many of Las Vegas's resort hotels now have spas that feature special premium treatments such as caviar facials. Of the larger resorts, the Venetian and Palms both have gorgeous spas, so may be good alternatives if you want a more central base than the Artisan.

Below: treading the boards at the Fashion Show Mall.

DISTANCE 5 miles (8km) round trip to Fashion Show Mall; 14 miles (23km) to Paris Las Vegas, the Rio, and back to the Artisan.
TIME A full day
START/END Artisan Hotel
POINTS TO NOTE
This route is done by car or taxi. The Artisan is just off the I-15 freeway at the Sahara exit; the Rio is also just off the freeway, at Flamingo Road exit. Both are on the west side of the freeway. Reserve ahead for the restaurants, spa treatments, and the Chippendales or *Le Rêve* (at least 30 days for the popular Chippendales).

After 1959, when the city built its original convention center, men started going off to Las Vegas on "business trips," leaving the women to look after the home front. Well, that was then; this is now. A recent survey revealed that female visitors to Las Vegas outnumber men by more than 8 per cent. Is that why lately the city has seen such rapid growth in spas, upscale shopping, and elegant light dining? Perhaps it's time to round up your gal pals and find out for yourselves.

This tour focuses on the off-Strip Artisan Hotel, which is small and intimate, and hence our pick as a base for a stylish girls' tour; plus it organizes daily wine-tastings at 4:30pm. The hotel is non-gaming, so a good choice if you are in need of a break from the bright lights and frenzy of the casino resorts. While the tastings are just for guests, note that the spa is not exclusive to hotel residents. If you are staying at another hotel, however, and would rather use the facilities there, simply revise the route accordingly.

SWIM AND BREAKFAST

Start the day in virtuous style, with a swim, then breakfast. If you opt to follow our tour to the letter, your day will begin at the boutique **Artisan**

Hotel ❶ (Artisan Hotel, 1501 West Sahara Avenue; tel: 702-214-4000 or 800-554-4092; www.theartisanhotel. com; *see p.115*). The hotel's Mediterranean-style pool, though not large, is lovely, with a fountain at one end. Wide day-beds, cabana tents, and small palms in terracotta pots surround it. Soothing music floats from the sound system, and food and beverage service from the hotel dining room is available poolside from 6am to 2pm.

FASHION SHOW MALL

Once calmed and sated, find out why many Las Vegas visitors today come not to gamble but to shop by heading for the **Fashion Show Mall ❷** (3200 Las Vegas Boulevard South; tel: 702-369-0704; Mon–Sat 10am–9pm, Sun 11am–7pm), on the northern stretch of the Strip. (From the Artisan, head east along West Sahara Avenue, make a right onto the Strip and continue until the Wynn Las Vegas is directly opposite. The Fashion Mall will be on your right.)

The City's Largest Mall

While there are a number of exceptional shopping areas in Strip resort hotels – the biggest and best include the Forum Shops in Caesars Palace *(see p.45)*, Le Boulevard in Paris Las Vegas *(see p.115)*, and the Grand Canal Shoppes in the Venetian *(see p.111)* – as well as several outlet malls *(see p.17)*, the stylish Fashion Show Mall is the city's largest. It is also the only mall that houses Macy's, Bloomingdale's, Nordstrom, Dillard's, Neiman Marcus,

and Saks Fifth Avenue under the same roof. There are also 187 other shops, from familiar high-street names to top-name designer boutiques and intimate Las Vegas originals, as well as about a dozen sit-down restaurants and a large third-floor international food court.

The mall hosts runway fashion shows every Fri, Sat, and Sun, hourly from noon to 6pm. After the midday fashion show, take time out for lunch at **Cafe Ba Ba Reeba!**, see 🍴①.

Above from far left: dummy fashions; make-up *(left)*, dress and handbags by Dior *(centre)*, and shopper *(right)* in the Fashion Show Mall.

Above: temptations on this tour: shopping and the Chippendales.

Food and Drink 🍴

① CAFÉ BA BA REEBA!
Fashion Show Mall – lower level east, 3200 Las Vegas Boulevard South; tel: 702-258-1811; Sun–Thur 11:30am–11pm, Fri–Sat 11:30am–midnight; $$

This big, colorful Spanish restaurant specializes in tapas – hot and cold appetizer-size plates – that run the gamut from seafood, meat, and fowl dishes to salads, cheeses, and vegetables. There are also several kinds of paella (rice with seafood), *calderos* (seafood or meat stews) and *brochetas* (seafood or meat skewers), but the best plan for groups is to order a tableful of tapas – two or three per person – and share them for a stunning culinary adventure. A typical spread for four might include a salad of endive, blue cheese, walnuts and *membrillo* (quince paste); a roasted tomato filled with ahi tuna; a plate of *salchichón* and chorizo sausages, serrano ham, and manchego cheese; marinated olives; deviled lobster; green beans and shallots; almond-and-herb-crusted chicken with romesco sauce; and goat cheese baked in tomato sauce.

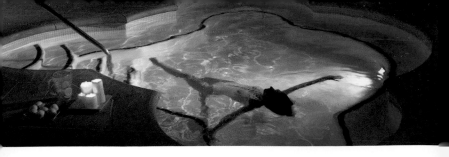

Above from left:
relax in one of Vegas's many luxury spas; Paris Las Vegas's Mon Ami Gabi restaurant does stylish French cuisine and has great views of the Bellagio's fountains.

Wine-Tasting
Complimentary tastings for guests are held daily at 4:30pm in the Artisan's cozy lounge, where more substantial servings of wine and cocktails are also available to those who want to get an early start on the evening's festivities.

CHOCOLATE BREAK

After lunch (perhaps for dessert, if you skipped this at Café Ba Ba Reeba!), consider a visit to **Ethel's Chocolate Lounge** (Fashion Show Mall, Lower level east; tel: 702-796-6662; Mon–Sat 10am–9pm, Sun 11am–7pm). While the Fashion Show Mall has several chocolate shops, the top pick for pure self-indulgence is this dessert café, a Las Vegas original where you can order Ethel's Chocolates by the piece, pairings of latte with four chocolates, or chocolate fondue with assorted dipping accompaniments. The specialty is sumptuous liqueur-filled chocolates.

SPA TREATMENT

At this point (probably now around mid-afternoon), head back to the Artisan (or to your own hotel, if you prefer) for a laze in the pool or a spa treatment. At the Artisan, massages are offered to day guests in the poolside

spa. If you are staying at the hotel, you can get nicely messy with the Artist's Palette Facial or the Mud Paint Body Wrap in the privacy of your room.

LADIES' NIGHT

To continue the tour into the evening, our suggestions still on a girly theme include an early dinner at **Mon Ami Gabi**, see ①② (at **Paris Las Vegas ❸**, 3655 Las Vegas Boulevard, at the southern end of the Strip, just after the crossroads with Flamingo Road, followed by a show by the Chippendales. For a more subtle alternative to the Chippendales, try *Le Rêve (see p.41).*

Chippendales
For the performance by the **Chippendales**, return to the crossroads of the Strip with Flamingo Road and take Flamingo Road past the Bellagio until you reach the **Rio All-Suite Las Vegas Hotel and Casino ❹** (3700 West Flamingo Road; tel: 702-252-7777;

Bright Lights
As of the last decade, there were 15,000 miles (21,140km) of neon on the Strip. The Rio's 125ft high marquee *(shown right)*, voted the city's best neon sign, uses 12,930ft of neon tubing and over 5,000 lightbulbs. Wasteful as some people consider it to be, the glare and glitter of this fantasy city in the desert is sacred to the casinos.

shows Sun–Thur 8:30pm, Sat 8:30 and 10:30pm).

These days, Las Vegas seems to have at least as many topless male body-builder shows for ladies only as it has topless showgirl shows. What makes this one special is that before and after the playfully sexy musical show, the dozen young male dancers circulate among audience members in the hotel's Flirt lounge, sporting an air of exaggerated chivalry. Once inside the theater, the spectators become much rowdier than a crowd of men would in a strip joint. This is one of the most popular shows in town, so be sure to get tickets early.

Food and Drink 🍴

② MON AMI GABI

Paris Las Vegas, 3655 Las Vegas Boulevard South; tel: 702-944-4224. Mon–Thur 11:30am–3:45pm, 4–11pm; Fri 11:30am–3:45pm, 4pm–midnight; Sat 11am–3:30pm, 4pm–midnight; Sun 11am–3:30pm, 4–11pm; $$–$$$

This gorgeous French restaurant – a spinoff from chef Gabino Sotelino's renowned French bistro in Chicago – faces out from a terrace overlooking the Strip in the shadow of the Eiffel Tower. Its wide sidewalk offers the most entertaining people-watching this side of the Champs-Elysées, and a fantastic view of the Bellagio fountain show (see p.112). There is also indoor seating with big picture windows and decor in a montage of French styles, but the outside tables are worth arriving early or waiting for. The fare includes seafood dishes such as trout Grenoblaise and skate, as well as lighter options such as salade Niçoise with grilled ahi tuna.

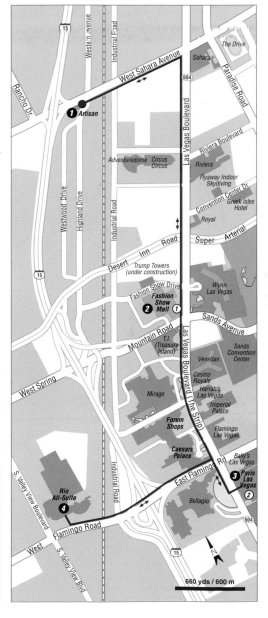

GAY LAS VEGAS

Outrageous Vegas has, perhaps, a surprisingly low-key and limited gay scene. Most GLBT visitors come for the same reasons as any other – the casinos, the shows, the Strip. But here are our suggestions if you want a bit of both worlds.

DISTANCE 8 miles (13km)
TIME A full day
START/END Blue Moon Resort
POINTS TO NOTE

This tour is best done by car or taxi. It is sensible to make reservations in advance at the Blue Moon Resort and buy tickets for *La Cage*.

In a city where the whole economy turns on the hospitality industry and the performing arts, you know there has got to be a large gay community. For many years, though, Las Vegas attitudes toward the lifestyle were ambivalent at best. Casino owners feared that a tolerant attitude might keep straights from coming to town and losing their money, even though the most successful head-

Lesbian Las Vegas

The scene for same-sex lovers in Vegas is not exclusively male-oriented. Lesbian bars and clubs are pretty much non-existent, but many gay hangouts host women-only sessions, so it is possible to find some action most nights of the week. The most popular bar for women is FreeZone (610 East Naples Drive; tel: 702-733-6701; 24 hrs), for women only on Tuesday nights. Flex Lounge (4371 West Charleston Boulevard; tel: 702-385-3539; 24 hrs) is a pool hall and dance club with a ladies-night (and female strippers) on Thursday, while the Backstreet Bar & Grill (5012 Arville Street; tel: 702-876-1844) hosts lesbian nights on Thursday. At weekends, Krave (3663 Las Vegas Boulevard South; tel: 702-836-0830; www.kravelasvegas.com) runs a girls-only "Bitch Bar" on Friday (from 9pm) and a GirlBar on alternate Saturdays. For more advice or for cultural or sports-oriented activities, Betty's Outrageous Adventures (tel: 702-991-9929; www.bettysout.com; small membership fee) is a group that organises social events from art gallery visits and movie nights to hikes through Red Rock Canyon and bowling evenings for lesbians (and their friends) in the Vegas area.

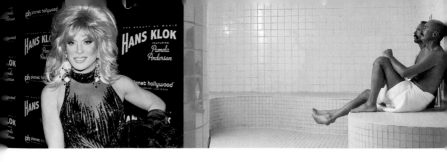

liners included Liberace and Siegfried and Roy. As recently as the 1960s, men convicted of homosexual acts were sentenced to the Nevada State Penitentiary, and raids on local gay clubs and bathhouses continued well into the 1980s.

Developments

But the situation started to change with astonishing speed in 1993, when Nevada's sodomy law was repealed. Within five years, the Las Vegas Metro Police Department became one of the first in the nation to adopt an anti-discrimination policy for hiring homosexual police officers, the Gay Pride Festival became a major annual fixture, and resorts began hosting gay events. Today, Las Vegas wedding chapels also offer gay and lesbian commitment ceremonies, and gay love in general has become much more tolerated within the straight community.

THE BLUE MOON

If you are staying at the gay-friendly **Blue Moon Resort** ❶ (2651 Westwood Drive; tel: 702-361-9099 or 866-796-9194; www.bluemoonlasvegas.com; *see also p.116*), take advantage of the complimentary continental breakfast – muffins, Danish, bagels, waffles, fresh fruit, and juices.

Follow this by some lazing by the lagoon-style swimming pool, which is surrounded by greenery, private cabanas, floating mattresses, and a (slightly) sandy beach area – not to mention a 10-ft (3-m) waterfall. Swimsuits are optional but not encouraged. If you are

not staying at the hotel, you can reach it by heading west off the Strip at its northern end; Westwood Drive is parallel to the main thoroughfare more or less on a level with Circus Circus (2880 Las Vegas Boulevard South; *see p.110*). Day passes are available.

FASHION SHOW MALL

The tour proper starts with a spot of shopping at the **Fashion Show Mall** ❷ (3200 Las Vegas Boulevard South; tel: 702-369-0704; Mon–Fri 10am–9pm, Sat 10am–8pm, Sun 11am–6pm), a short taxi ride or a hot 20-minute walk from the Blue Moon Resort. The mall is visited on the previous tour *(see p.57)*, but in terms of its appeal to a gay audience, it consistently wins the Best of Gay Vegas Award for Best Shopping as voted for by the readership of *QVegas* magazine's annual *Qrific*.

Above from far left: Betty's; sexy classic statue; celebrated Joan Rivers impersonator, Frank Rivers; relaxing in a spa.

Information Hub
The Gay and Lesbian Center (953 East Sahara Avenue, Suite B 25; tel: 702-733-9800; www.the centerlv.com; Mon–Fri 11am–7pm, Sat 10am–3pm) provides plenty of information including a guide to local gay and gay-friendly bars.

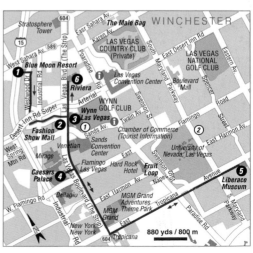

WYNN LAS VEGAS

Now cross over the Strip towards **Wynn Las Vegas** ❸ (3131 Las Vegas Boulevard South; tel: 701-693-7871; *see also pp.40 and 111*), directly opposite the Fashion Show Mall, where the Wynn Esplanade boasts shops belonging to Oscar de la Renta and Jean-Paul Gaultier. The Wynn Las Vegas is tycoon Steve Wynn's latest project (following hot on the heels of the Mirage and the Bellagio) and its no-expense-spared decor offers proof that Las Vegas Strip megaresorts don't have to be tacky. You might want to gamble in the casino or just stroll through the common areas

of this elegantly trendy hotel, spotting the billionaire's original paintings and sculptures that are scattered through the common areas, and which put most art museums' collections to shame. For lunch, and a spot of beautiful people-watching try **Alex**, see ⑪①.

CAESARS PALACE

For more shopping, continue south up the Strip to **Caesars Palace** ❹ (3570 Las Vegas Boulevard South; tel: 702-731-7110; open Sun–Thur 10am–11pm, Fri–Sat 10am–midnight; *see also pp.44, 78, and 112*). The resort's Forum Shops forms one of the most exclusive

Pride Week
In 2003, the mayor of Las Vegas officially proclaimed the first full week of May to be Pride Week. The Southern Nevada Association of Pride. Inc. (SNAPI, 5015 West Sahara Avenue; tel: 702-615-9429; www.lasvegaspride. org) sponsors a full schedule of parades, parties, art shows, and dances on the Strip and the Fruit Loop *(see p.64)* and in the 18b Arts District *(see p.38)*. Thousands of participants celebrate the change from the repressive era of 1983, when fewer than 200 people showed up, risking arrest, at the first Gay Pride Day in Sunset Park.

Right: bare-faced cheek at a cabaret.

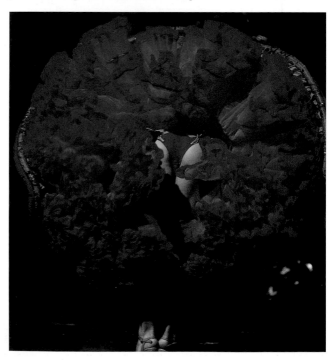

shopping zones in the US, and there's something irresistible about juxtaposing designer boutiques with all those marble columns and outsized statues of Michelangelo's *David* and other nude Italians.

LIBERACE MUSEUM

Drive or taxi along to the southern end of the Strip, then turn east onto East Tropicana Avenue. This brings you to the recently renovated and expanded **Liberace Museum ⑤** (1775 East Tropicana Avenue; tel: 702-798-5595; www.liberace.org; Tue–Sat 10am–5pm, Sun noon–4pm; charge; NB: visitors who arrive by taxi or bus can show their receipts and get a $2 discount on admission), where the property and personal effects of old-time Las Vegas's king of high camp are on display. Among the over-the-top memorabilia is a gold-filigree grand piano, the world's largest rhinestone, and stage outfits that would make Elton John blush, as well as collections of the entertainer's cars, jewelry, and of course, his trademark candelabras.

Lowdown on Liberace

Born into a musical family in 1919, it soon became clear that Walter Valentino Liberace also had musical talent. At the age of 14, he soloed with the Chicago Symphony, but by the time he was 21 he had dropped his first two names and began appearing in clubs simply as "Liberace." He also got breaks on the silver screen and on television, so that when Liberace opened in Vegas at the

Riviera *(see pp.64 and 110)* in 1955, he became the highest paid entertainer in the city's history. Unbelievable as it may be, Liberace denied that he was gay throughout his life, even after his longtime male lover sued him for palimony, and the entertainer brought libel actions against journalists who hinted that he was. Following his death from an Aids-related illness in 1987,

Out In Print

A wealth of print media, available at the Blue Moon Resort, and many other locations around town, helps visitors and residents get in touch with Las Vegas's GLBT community. The city's original gay underground newspaper, the *Vegas Gay Times*, started publication very secretly in 1979 and later became the *Nevada Gay Times*, then the *Las Vegas Bugle*. Today, no longer underground, it has evolved into *QVegas*, a slick monthly magazine (www.qvegas.com). Both it and *Out Las Vegas* (www.outlasvegas.com) are published by Stonewall Publishing, Inc. (2408 Pardee Place; tel: 702-650-0636). The Lambda Business & Professional Association (953 ER. Sahara Avenue B-25; tel: 702-593-2875; www. lambdalv.com) sponsors a free membership directory, the 225-page *Las Vegas' Gay & Lesbian Community Yellow Pages* (tel: 702-737-7701; www.vegasgayyellowpages.com), put out by the publishers of *Las Vegas Night Beat* (1140 Almond Tree Lane; tel: 702-369-8441).

Above from far left: hunky Centurian at Caesars Palace; Liberace and piano.

Above from left:
Paymon's Mediter-
ranean Café; Frank
Marino as Joan
Rivers; golf with a
spectacular back-
drop; the dice girls,
the original showgirls.

Liberace's manager revealed why: if his fans knew, Liberace once confided, "that's all they'll remember about me." So he stayed in the closet – but what a closet! Before you leave the neigh-borhood, peek into neighboring **Carluccio's Tivoli Gardens**, a classic Italian restaurant that was originally designed and owned by the glittering maestro himself.

A better option for dinner is **Paymon's Mediterranean Café**, see ⑪②. From the museum drive west on East Tropicana Avenue, then turn right at South Maryland Parkway and head north. The cafe is on your right, just before the junction with Flamingo Road, opposite the UNLV campus.

LA CAGE

To continue the themed tour into the evening, our recommendation is a per-formance of *La Cage* at the **Riviera** ❻ (2901 Las Vegas Boulevard South; tel: 702-734-5110; shows Wed–Mon 7:30pm; *see p.110*). The hotel is at the northern end of the Strip, so you will need to head back the way you came, continuing down the Strip after Wynn Las Vegas for a couple of blocks.

Female Impersonators

A Las Vegas classic, this long-running female-impersonator show emceed by the legendary Frank Marino as Joan Rivers has been running for more than 20 years. It presents America's top drag performers and covers all the old standbys such as Barbra, Bette, Judy, Cher, and Celine, as well as a few sur-prises such as Michael Jackson and a comically obese Madonna. The inti-mate theater offers audience members a close-up look. Note: the manage-ment goes out of its way to make sure it is perceived as an illusion show, not a gay show; it has been known for male couples to be ejected from perform-ances for "public displays of affection" – hand-holding.

THE FRUIT LOOP

After the show, head to Paradise Road between Harmon Avenue and Naples Street. This compact area, the main cruising zone in Vegas, contains a gay bookstore and diverse all-night gay bars and cafes including **Buffalo** (4640 Paradise Road; tel: 702-733-8355); **Free Zone** (610 East Naples Street; tel: 702-794-2300); **8½** (4633 Paradise Road; tel: 702-731-1919); **Gipsy** (4605 Paradise Road, tel: 702-731-1919); and **Suede** (3640 Paradise Road #4; tel 702-791-3463).

Food and Drink

② PAYMON'S MEDITERRANEAN CAFÉ

4147 South Maryland Parkway; tel: 702-731-6030; www.paymons.com; Mon–Thur 11am–1am, Fri–Sat 11am–3am; $$

This award-winning, gay-friendly Las Vegas favorite serves excellent Greek, Persian, and Indian fare such as *pastitsio*, *spanakopita*, *fesenjan*, and chicken tandoori, as well as various steak, lamb, chicken, fish, and vegetable kabobs. Decor is unpretentious in the restaurant and Arabian-Nights fabulous in the adjoining Hookah Lounge with its dramatic lighting, art-cov-ered walls, popular happy hour (Mon–Sat 5–7pm), and water pipes on every table. (They burn a tasty herbal mixture to side-step Las Vegas's ban on smoking tobacco in public places.) Paymon's supports the St. Therese Center Dining Out for Life fundraising program to fight Aids.

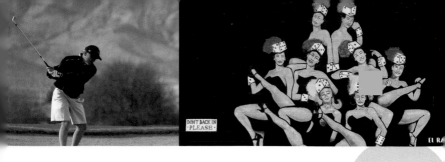

VEGAS FOR THE BOYS

Of course not everyone visits Vegas for designer boutiques and Liberace tribute acts. For more traditional hedonists, Sin City's less touchy-feely attractions include babes, betting and booze. There are sports options, too, from golf to billiards, plus guns, and cigars.

Though the glitz, the glamor, and the gambling are huge draws, people choose Vegas for many reasons. And since the 1960s Vegas has played on its reputation as a place where the men could escape to find girls and behave badly. Over the years, the image has gone from seediness to caricature, with the sex industry sitting at times uncomfortably next to the family-friendly resorts and swanky corporate hotels: in a city in which everything is done to excess, the relationship with sex is a fragile one. Still, Vegas attracts its fair share of men looking for pleasure – and an increasingly number of men on stag weekends – and this tour is aimed (within reason) to appeal to that more macho audience.

SPORTING START

Begin the day bright and early with a game of golf with friends – or, if this doesn't appeal, with a pool or bowling session *(see right)*. The closest non-members' golf course to the Strip is the **Wynn Golf and Country Club** ❶ (tel: 888-320-7122; www.wynnlas vegas.com; hotel guests only), located right behind the hotel, although note that only hotel guests are permitted to use this course.

DISTANCE 8 miles (13km)
TIME A full day
START Various
END The Tropicana
POINTS TO NOTE
Start/end points vary according to whether you start with golf, pool, or bowling. Don't even think about drinking and driving, so do this tour on foot or by taxi or monorail. Make reservations for dinner at Legends and for the Folies Bergère or comedy nights.

If you are not staying at the Wynn, the nearest public course to the Strip is the nearby 18-hole **Las Vegas National Golf Club** ❷ (1911 East Desert Inn Road; tel: 702-734-1796; www.lasvegasnational.americangolf. com), which sits between East Desert Inn Road and South Eastern Avenue. Studded with tall palms and pines, this challenging course was formerly the home of the PGA Las Vegas Invitational and also hosts other PGA and LPGA events.

Pool and Bowling
If you're not a golfer, "sporting" alternative ways to spend the morning include playing pool at **Pink E's** ❸

Above: attractions on the Vegas for the Boys tour.

Smoking and the Law

If you buy "Havana" cigars, be advised that since the beginning of 2007, it has been illegal to smoke tobacco in any indoor public place in the greater Las Vegas area. The only exception is casinos – not casino bars, only the casinos themselves.

(3695 West Flamingo Road; tel: 702-252-4666; 24 hrs), west of the Strip. There are 50 tables here, but bring your sunglasses, as they are pink.

Another alternative is bowling: the nearest facility to the Strip is at **Lucky Strike Lanes** at the **Rio All-Suite Las Vegas Hotel and Casino ❹** (3700 West Flamingo Road; tel: 702-252-7777; charge), a ten-lane facility in the Rio. It has a bar and full-service restaurant, with a weekend buffet, on the premises. (Note that after 9pm, children and youths under 21 are not allowed, and the lights dim to create an atmosphere more like that of a night-club than a bowling alley.)

GIRLS AND GUNS

After your game, athletic or otherwise, you probably feel you've earned lunch. A popular choice with the boys is the questionably named **Hooters**, see ⑪①,

at 115 East Tropicana Avenue, a hotel that seems to be staffed entirely by young women in bikinis and sarongs. You can also gamble here if you want to.

Gun Store

After lunch, turn up the testosterone and head eastwards to the one-of-a-kind **Gun Store ❺** (2900 Tropicana Avenue; tel: 702-454-1110; daily 9am–6:30pm). Here, you can rent a real machine gun – your choice of an Uzi, an M-16, a Thompson sub or an M3A1 Grease Gun, among others – and blaze away at human-shaped targets until your adrenalin is pumped to the max. Monitor your progress, though, as you can spend a fortune paying for ammunition – an Uzi can empty a clip in under a second. Note that Tuesday is Ladies Day, when women shoot for free.

CIGAR COMPANY

Next stop is the **Havana Cigar Company ❻** (3900 Paradise Road; tel: 702-892-9555; Sun–Thur 10am–10pm, Fri–Sat 10am–11pm), reached by making a left from Tropicana on to Paradise Road and heading north.

As it is illegal to buy or smoke Cuban cigars in the US, this store and cigar bar sells primarily lookalike Cohibas, Partagas, La Auroras, and Romeo y Julietas imported from the Dominican Republic, the world's largest cigar-producing nation. Counterfeits? Probably, but some cigar buffs outside the US who have access to the real thing claim the Dominicans make

better ones. Havana Cigar has a private club cigar and wine bar.

THE TROPICANA

Our recommendations for the evening are based at the **Tropicana** ❼ (115 East Tropicana Avenue; tel: 702-739-2222 or 800-829-9034; *see p.115*). Start with a meal at **Legends**, see ⑪②, followed by saucy French-style topless Folies Bergère or a rather less glamorous – but hopefully no less engaging – comedy show.

Folies Bergère

The most popular show in Las Vegas history, the **Folies Bergère** (Tropicana, 115 East Tropicana Avenue; tel: 702-739-2222 or 800-829-9034; shows Mon, Wed, Thur, Sat 7:30pm and

10pm; Tue, Fri 8:30pm; *see p.11*) originated in Paris almost 140 years ago and was brought to the Tropicana in 1959, scandalizing Sin City with the first topless showgirls in the US. It has been playing here ever since, changing, growing, and maintaining its reputation for sexy flamboyance. The 7:30pm shows are all described as "family-friendly," whereas the later shows are full-on tits-and-glitz.

Comedy

For those in search of more humorous entertainment, an alternative to the Folies Bergère is **Comedy Stop at the Trop** (tel: 702-739-2714; www. comedystop.com; shows nightly 8pm and 10:30pm). Some of the best comedians in the country show what they're made of at this adults-only club.

Above: bowling and booze.

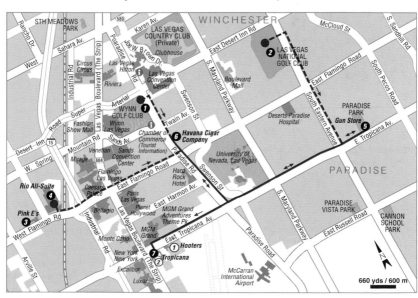

ROMANTIC LAS VEGAS

Vegas is a magnet for romantics who favor a different type of scene. Be it elopement, engagement, honeymoon, commitment vows, marriage or illicit affair – Las Vegas loves lovers.

DISTANCE 40 miles (64km)

TIME A full day (including dinner and show)

START Ritz-Carlton

END Mandalay Bay

POINTS TO NOTE

There are several things to organize in advance with this tour: make spa reservations as far ahead as possible and buy *Zumanity* tickets weeks in advance; make reservations (timed for sunset) at the Top of the World two weeks or more in advance; and hire a limousine at least one day before you plan to do the tour. "Smart-casual" dress, meaning a jacket for men and no jeans and trainers, is required for our dinner recommendation.

On Bended Knee

Lovers who plan to top off the evening by popping the question may find the perfect spot on the observation deck of the Eiffel Tower at Paris Las Vegas (3655 Las Vegas Boulevard South; tel: 702-946-7000; www.parislasvegas. com), where an area is set aside for just that purpose. The hotel offers various marriage proposal packages, with the pricier ones including champagne, long-stemmed roses, and a photographer to record the occasion.

Above from far left: big day for a young, hip bride and groom; Cupid's Wedding Chapel; Vegas hugs; cupid's arrow at one of the city's many wedding chapels.

Food and Drink 🍴

① **POOLSIDE BAR & GRILL**

Ritz-Carlton – Lake Las Vegas; 1610 Lake Las Vegas Parkway, Henderson; tel: 702-567-4700; www. ritzcarlton.com; mid-spring–mid-fall; 11am–sunset; $$

Cool off in the pool, then dine while you dry (towels are not essential in the desert sun). This cafe serves sandwich wraps, salads, smoothies and other healthy fare, as well as festive drinks.

Las Vegas has less than half a percent of the US population, yet it is the location of choice for five percent of all the country's marriage ceremonies. And although it is actually statistically quite rare for couples who have come to Vegas just for fun to get drunk and wake up to find themselves unexpectedly married, myths of this kind are certainly the stuff of American situation comedies and cheesy films. That would never happen to you, of course, but the mere possibility adds a special tingle to romance in Las Vegas. Regardless, whether you're pondering the idea of taking your partner home to meet the folks; or you've already bought the ring in anticipation of the perfect moment to pop the question; or you have just noticed what a great smile your spouse of 20 years has, when such a moment comes along, spare no expense.

RITZ-CARLTON

Breakfast in bed is a wonderful way to start a romantic day, and for a particularly lovey-dovey time, spend the night outside of is Sin City at the **Ritz-Carlton** ① (1610 Lake Las Vegas Parkway, Henderson; tel: 702-567-4700; www.ritzcarlton. com; *see also p.117)*. Don't count on a lie in here, as a clock tower nearby starts

chiming out the hours from 7am and golfers, who make up a large part of the hotel's clientele, often get up early in the morning and make noise in the hallways. Just call room service, which can serve you such tantalizing breakfasts as baked malted waffles with caramelized pineapple.

Lake Las Vegas

After breakfast, head outside to the man-made **Lake Las Vegas**. (Start the tour here if you are not actually staying at the hotel.) There's a paved public walkway around the lake and the Ritz-Carlton has its own sandy beach (with kayaks and bicycles available to rent for guests). The more ambitious will find hiking trails running from the hotel into the surrounding vast, empty desert. In summer, the early morning sun warms the dry air fast: by 9:30, it may drive you back inside the air-conditioned hotel. Another option is a visit to the nearby MonteLago "village" with its quaint, cobblestone streets lined with chic shops.

Spa

If you are hungry, head back to the hotel, for a bite at the **Poolside Bar & Grill**, see ⑪①. Follow this with a spot of relaxation in the whirlpool by the waterfalls, then drip in the steam room, and simmer in the sauna. There are separate facilities for men and women, but the spa has treatment rooms for couples. Hot stone massage, aromatherapy massage, and a full menu of other body-healing pleasures are available to couples for an addi-

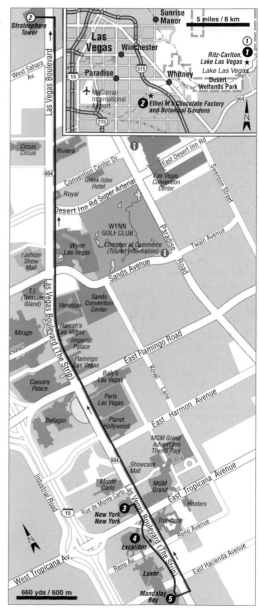

Stretch Limos
Las Vegas must have more stretch limos per capita than anyplace else in the Western Hemisphere. They can be rented by the hour, and compared to most Las Vegas thrill rides, are not really that expensive. Among the numerous limousine services in town are: Celebrity Coaches, tel: 702-736-649, www.celebritylas vegas.com; Highroller Limos, tel: 702-868-5600, www.high rollerlimo.com; Life of Sin Limo, tel: 702-792-6666; Presidential Limousine, tel: 702-731-5577, www. presidentiallimolv. com; and Imagine Vegas, tel: 866-220-3343, www.imagine vegas.com.

tional \$25 above the regular price. You can also lounge together on the spa's sundecks and in the garden.

CHOCOLATE TOUR

After lunch, it is time to head off to **Ethel M's Chocolate Factory and Botanical Gardens ❷** (2 Cactus Garden Drive; tel: 702–458-8864; www.ethelschocolate.com; 8:30am–7pm; free). The chocolate factory is off Sunset Road in the town of Henderson, on your way from Lake Las Vegas to the Strip.

Scientists may not yet have proven that chocolate is unquestionably an aphrodisiac, but you can investigate for yourselves by visiting this premier

Food and Drink 🍴
② TOP OF THE WORLD RESTAURANT
Stratosphere Tower, 2000 Las Vegas Boulevard South; tel: 702-380-7777; daily 11am–3pm, Sun–Thur 5:30–10:30pm, Fri–Sat 5:30–11pm; \$\$\$
There are few places as romantic as a revolving restaurant, and the Las Vegas Strip has one of the best. Perched 800ft (244m) in the air on the tallest structure on the Las Vegas Strip, this restaurant revolves 360 degrees every 80 minutes. Time your reservations to coincide with sunset for the take-your-breath-away experience of watching the Strip light up before your eyes. It is so fabulous it can even overshadow the menu that features delicacies like lobster and crab ravioli, Muscovy duck, and Colorado rack of lamb. Try the Chocolate Stratosphere filled with mouth-watering Belgium chocolate mousse for desert.

gourmet chocolate maker *(see p.58)* for a self-guided factory tour (including free samples), and a stroll in the desert gardens with their spiky cacti.

CAVIAR AND VODKA

Continue into central Las Vegas and park your car (if driving) at the casino at **New York New York ❸** (3790 Las Vegas Boulevard South; *see also pp.46, 88, and 115*); leave it there until you're ready to return to your hotel. Cross the street to the **Excalibur ❹**, where you can catch the free monorail tram past the Luxor to the **Mandalay Bay ❺** (3950 Las Vegas Boulevard South; tel: 702-632-7404; Sun–Thur 5–11pm; *see also pp.35, 46, and 114*). Your first destination is **Red Square**, the hotel's Russian-themed restaurant and bar, which has more than 100 kinds of premium vodka chilling in its freezer vault. Fur coats and hats are provided for the sub-zero temperatures. When you enter the vault, you find a bar of solid ice and a fantastic contrast to the desert heat outside the hotel.

EVENING OPTIONS

If this has set you up for a memorable dinner, our suggestion for an unusual meal out is the Stratosphere Tower's **Top of the World Restaurant**, see 🍴② *(see also p.53)*, although to get there, you need to head all the way down the Strip. One option for this is to hire a stretch limo – all those you see cruising up and down the Strip are for rent by the hour. If you make

arrangements well in advance *(see left)*, you can have one waiting for you at the Mandalay to take you to the restaurant. Or, just take a taxi down the Strip and order a limousine to pick you up after your meal.

These limos are as luxurious inside as most hotel rooms, with built-in televisions, sound systems, minibars, and sofa-style seats that wrap around the interior. You'll probably have a one-hour minimum rental, so have the driver cruise up and down the Strip until your time is up.

Zumanity at New York New York

After dinner, head back to **New York New York** *(see opposite)* at the southern end of the Strip if you want to continue the themed tour with the 10:30pm showing of *Zumanity* (tel: 702-740-6815 or 866-606-7111; shows Tue–Sat 7:30pm and 10:30pm; over 18 only).

Of the five Cirque du Soleil shows on the Strip, this one is by far the most sensual, blending burlesque, cabaret, acrobatics, and special effects, with a few naughty bits. The atmospherically lit show includes seductive versions of traditional circus skills such as contortion and aerial stunts, along with dance styles that range from flamenco and tango to African dance, Viennese waltz, and even striptease, and is a fitting end to this romantic tour.

Above from far left: looking out from the Stratosphere Tower; exterior of the tower; celebrate with a Vegas cocktail; Lovers Lane

Below: *Zumanity*, at New York New York.

OLD WEST LAS VEGAS

Go off the beaten track and you will find that Vegas has history, too: this all-day adventure reveals the Las Vegas Valley's pioneer years as an oasis for farming and ranching in the harsh Mojave Desert.

DISTANCE 65 miles (105km)
TIME A full day
START Golden Gate Hotel
END The Hideaway
POINTS TO NOTE

This route is best done by car, preferably an air-conditioned one. Make an early start, heading off by 9:30am, earlier if possible. If you want to do a sunset trail ride in Red Rock Canyon (note that this is fairly expensive), book as far ahead as you can.

Las Vegas became a railroad town when it was chosen as a stopping point for trains. Then, cowboys came to the saloons on Fremont Street for much the same kind of recreation that is offered by casinos to visitors today. As you spend time Downtown, you'll no doubt see authentic Westerners from Montana, Wyoming, and Idaho towns, where most commercial flights from the local airports go to Las Vegas, as well as many who make their homes in the vast, mostly empty landscape that surrounds Sin City.

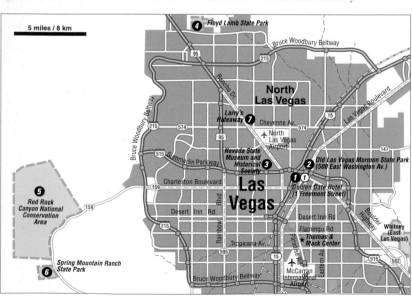

GOLDEN GATE HOTEL

If you want an Old West style hotel, try the **Golden Gate Hotel** ❶ (1 Fremont Street; tel: 702-385-1906 or 800-426-1906; www.goldengatecasino. com; *see also p.116)*. Make an early start with breakfast at the hotel's **Bay City Diner**, see ⑪①.

OLD LAS VEGAS MORMON FORT STATE PARK

From the hotel, follow North Main Street north-east to Washington Avenue; turn right and drive about four blocks to the intersection with North Las Vegas Boulevard and **Old Las Vegas Mormon State Park** ❷ (500 East Washington Avenue; tel: 702-486-3511; http://parks.nv.gov/olvmf. htm; daily 8am–4:30pm; charge), the first main stop on today's tour.

Old Mormon Fort

Within the park is one of Nevada's most venerable buildings, the Old

Mormon Fort, built to protect missionaries and settlers en route to California. Inside the high adobe walls, a reconstructed tower overlooks a plaza deserted except for a broken-down wagon and the iron pegs for throwing horseshoes.

The only surviving part of the original structure is the building nearest to the little creek, rising from underground aquifers a few miles west. These supplied a water source running through the fort, nourishing the poor

Above from far left: Golden Gate Casino; dinosaurs at the Nevada State Museum; a new take on old-West fashion; classic method of transportation.

Below: mapping Downtown, the historic area of Vegas.

Food and Drink 🍴

① BAY CITY DINER

Golden Gate Hotel, 1 Fremont Street; tel: 702-385-1906; Tue–Thur 6am–2am, Fri–Sun 24hr; $

This is an old-fashioned spot in the Golden Gate Hotel, with vintage diner decor comprising red Naugahyde booths, black-and-white checkerboard floor, and gleaming stainless steel fixtures. It features inexpensive all-American fare, including a very good steak and eggs breakfast. Get here early – there's often a line to get in.

Above from left:
old-style roulette
wheel; Floyd Lamb
State Park.

soil in which the hopeful missionaries planted crops including potatoes, tomatoes, and squash. Some of these same plants are grown today in the museum's demonstration garden.

After the Mormons left, a miner named Octavius Gass acquired the site along with other land to assemble a sizable ranch – the first in the region. He also opened a general store and blacksmith shop. It was then bought by Archibald Steward, whose widow Helen ran the ranch after her husband was killed in 1884 and later sold the property to the railroad. The site on which the Stewart home stood is scheduled for excavation to unearth any secrets that may lie buried beneath.

Pro Rodeo's "Superbowl"

The biggest cowboy event of the year in Las Vegas, the National Finals Rodeo has been held at the Thomas & Mack Center in Las Vegas every December since 1985. The 10-day event draws upward of 140,000 spectators each year to watch the top professional rodeo athletes in the US and Canada compete in saddle bronc riding, bareback bronc riding, bull riding, calf roping, team roping, steer wrestling, and barrel racing. Tickets are very hard to get. A lottery is held one year in advance, and only one out of 25 people who enter actually get tickets. There is a second lottery for balcony seating 10 months ahead. To try for a ticket, contact Wrangler National Finals Rodeo, c/o Thomas & Mack Center, 4505 South Maryland Parkway, Box 450005, Las Vegas, Nevada 89154-0005; www.nfrexperience.com. Tickets are often available over the Internet from vendors who buy blocks of tickets to resell individually at a profit, for instance, First Choice Tickets, Inc., 17547 Ventura Boulevard, Suite 102, Encino, CA 91316; tel: 888-637-7633; www.nfr-rodeo.com.

NEVADA STATE MUSEUM AND HISTORICAL SOCIETY

Next stop is the **Nevada State Museum and Historical Society ❸** (333 South Valley View Boulevard; daily 9am–5pm; charge). Until recently this small museum was set on a lake in Lorenzi Park, off Washington Avenue 3 miles (5km) due west of the Old Mormon Fort, but moved to new premises fewer than 2 miles (1km) away, next door to the Las Vegas Springs Preserve on Valley View Boulevard, west of Downtown. Twice the size of its old home, this new museum showcases contains historical exhibits on the Las Vegas area from pioneer days through World War II, as well as fossils, and stuffed and mounted specimens of present-day Mojave desert fauna.

FLOYD LAMB STATE PARK

By now it should be around noon, time for a spot of lunch at the **Floyd Lamb State Park ❹** at Tule Springs (9200 Tule Springs Road; tel: 702-486-5413; daily 6am–7pm; charge per vehicle). This is located 15 miles (24km) north of Downtown Las Vegas off US Highway 95 (take exit 93 – Durango Drive – and follow the signs). You can pick up picnic fixings near the park at Albertsons supermarket (8410 Farm Road; tel: 702-658-2030) or, for something a little more exotic, the Taste of Asian Market (7501 North Cimarron Street; tel: 702-396-4143).

The park is named after late state

senator Floyd Lamb, who was instrumental in getting the land transferred to the state in 1977. Six years later, Lamb was convicted of soliciting a $20,000 bribe from an undercover FBI agent, and the authorities have been trying without success to have his name removed from the park ever since. Guided carriage tours are available within the park *(see right)*.

Historic Site

This 2,040-acre (825-hectare) park occupies the site of Tule Springs, a large desert oasis that was a stopping place for nomadic Indian hunters and, later on, explorers and prospectors. Farmer Bert Nay bought water rights to the springs and started a small farm here in 1916. It was expanded into a working cattle ranch in 1941, and, during the late 1940s, was converted into a dude ranch, where women stayed while establishing Nevada residency to take advantage of the state's liberal divorce laws.

The Park Today

Today, several buildings from the former ranch still remain, along with the descendants of the peacocks that strolled the lawns during the ranch's heyday. Most of the park is natural desert, with three fishing ponds (a Nevada fishing license is required if you want to fish) fed by the springs.

Carriage Tours
In Floyd Lamb State Park, guided carriage tours take visitors to the remains of one of the Las Vegas area's earliest ranches and an archeological dig, where archaic Native American relics and relics of fossils of prehistoric mammals have been discovered.

Below: cowboys enjoying the Rodeo.

Above: scenes from the canyon.

Open-Air Theater
Topping the list of local performing arts in the summer months, Super Summer Theatre presents Broadway plays under the stars in Red Rock Canyon. Three different plays run three weeks each, Wed–Sun with performances at 8pm. For schedule and tickets, call 702-594-7529 or visit www.supersummer theatre.com.

Right: if your budget allows, splash out on a horse ride.

Picnic tables with grills surround the ponds. The springs area is also known as one of Nevada's major fossil quarries, where remains of mammoths, giant camels and sloths, miniature horses, and giant condors have been found. Note that many of these fossils can be viewed at the **Las Vegas Natural History Museum** (900 North Las Vegas Boulevard; 702-384-3466; daily 9am– 4pm; charge).

RED ROCK CANYON

To reach **Red Rock Canyon** ❺ take Durango Drive to County Road 215 (also known as the Bruce Woodbury Beltway). Go south for 10 miles (16km) to exit 22, Charleston Boulevard/Red Rock Canyon. Follow West Charleston Boulevard (Nevada Highway 159) for 5 miles (8km) until you pass the Red Rock Canyon entrance (Scenic Drive). Stay on the main highway for another 5 miles (8km), until you reach Spring Mountain Ranch.

Spring Mountain Ranch

The **Spring Mountain Ranch** ❻ (Red Rock Canyon National Conservation Area; tel: 702-875-4141; daily 10am–4pm; guided tours daily noon, 1 and 2pm, Sat–Sun 3pm; charge) dates back to 1876, when it was named Sand Stone Ranch. When the original owner died, he left it to two Paiute orphan boys whom he had adopted. The ranch later passed through the

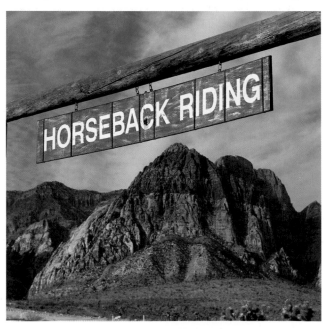

RED ROCK CANYON
National Conservation Area

hands of several celebrity owners, including Hollywood furrier Willard George and the billionaire recluse Howard Hughes.

Guided and self-guided tours take in the original cabin, the mansion-like main house, the cemetery, the black-smith shop, horse barn and corrals, and a facility where Willard George used to farm chinchillas. Docents lead guided tours during the early after-noon and are on hand to answer questions the rest of the time.

Cowboy Trail Rides

If your budget allows and you've booked well in advance, at around 5pm it is time for a sunset horseride and barbecue at Red Rock Canyon (Cowboy Trail Rides, Red Rock Canyon; tel: 702-477-0835; www.mountcharlestonriding stables.com; hours vary seasonally; charge; reservations essential).

A 90-minute guided horseback ride takes you through the narrows of Red Rock canyon floor, then up to Over-look Summit, where you can watch the sun set and the lights of Las Vegas come on in the distance. Then it's back to camp for a chuckwagon steak dinner, and, afterward, you can roast marsh-mallows and s'mores (marshmallows, roasted with chocolate, and sand-wiched between wafers) over the campfire, listen to some tales and his-tory, and sing along to cowboy songs.

If playing at cowboys does not appeal, head back into central Vegas and choose a restaurant from the Directory section of the guide *(see pp.118–23).*

THE HIDEAWAY

Real cowboys and cowgirls in the Las Vegas area go to **Larry's Hideaway** ❼ (3369 Thorn Boulevard; tel: 702-645-1899; daily 24hrs), a huge country & western dance club with a small menu of bar food in an otherwise rather des-olate area of north Las Vegas. To get here from Red Rock Canyon, retrace your route until you're going north-bound on County Road 215. If you haven't heard any singing cowboys lately, be sure to come here on a Wednesday evening for karaoke night.

Above from far left: admiring the views; entrance to the conservation area.

Cowboy Threads

In Las Vegas, you can wear boots and a cowboy hat in the most exclusive resort hotels in town – including most restaurants that have dress codes – without feeling out of place. Visitors, both men and women, who find themselves in need of Western apparel will find great selections at Sheplers Western Wear (3025 East Tropicana Avenue; tel: 702-898-3000 – the most conveniently located of three branches of Sheplers in Vegas) and Cowtown Boots (1080 East Flamingo Road; tel: 702-737-8469). During the National Finals Rodeo, more than 400 vendors sell western wear at Cowboy Christmas, a public gift show held in the Las Vegas Convention Center.

GAMBLERS' LAS VEGAS

Lured by Lady Luck, gamblers are glued to the slot machines whatever the time of day – or night. Here, we demystify the casino experience and introduce the range of gaming distractions on offer, for example, at Caesars Palace.

DISTANCE N/A – the whole day is spent at Caesars Palace
TIME Around 7 hours for the casino tour and free lessons
START/END Caesars Palace
POINTS TO NOTE
The first free lesson is at 11am, but it is best to arrive early (say 10am), if you want to sit at the table instead of watching from the sidelines.

Below: the slots: the most popular way to gamble in Las Vegas.

For serious gamblers, a trip to Las Vegas requires no detailed itinerary. Simply check into your favorite hotel – most likely a Downtown hotel, where there are fewer touristic distractions than on the Strip. Then head directly to the casino's cashier cage, invest in a tray of chips, and you're on your way.

But Las Vegas visitors who are new to the world of casino gambling often arrive with daydreams of breaking the bank. Maybe you have a special $20 bill that came from some friend or relative who asked you to bet their birth date at the roulette table. The reality is, first-timers usually lack the confidence to test their luck at casino tables and, instead, settle for a few not-very-exciting hours of watching their stake dribble away a quarter at a time in slot machines. Here is a painless plan to help you fathom the world of casinos. *(For more gambling tips, see pp.18–19.)*

BREAKFAST AND A TOUR

Start with breakfast at around 9am. If at **Caesars Palace** (3570 Las Vegas Boulevard South; tel: 702-731-7110 or 800-634-6661; www.caesars.com; *see pp.44, 62, and 112)*, a good place is the **Augustus Cafe**, see ⑪①.

In Caesars Palace, or any other Las Vegas gaming hotel, visitors have no

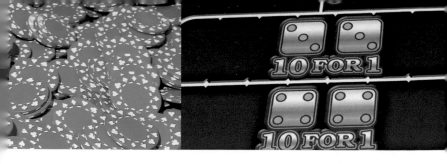

Above from far left:
some of what to
expect in a casino.

problem finding the casino. It is
centrally located, so much so that you
have to make your way through it to
reach the reception desk, the swimming pool, the restaurants, the front
door, or even the elevator to your room.
Caesars Palace has three casino areas,
totaling 149,000sq ft (13,845sq m),
surrounding the oldest of the hotel's
guest room towers.

SLOT MACHINES

The first thing you'll notice is that the
casino is full of slot machines, the most
popular casino games by a wide
margin. A recent survey by the owners
of Caesars Palace reveals that 66 per
cent of men and 81 per cent of women
play the slots rather than table games:
they're simple, and you don't have to
interact with a dealer or other players.

The Odds

However, they also generally offer the
worst odds in the casino. By Nevada
state law, slot machines must pay out
at least 75 per cent of the money played
in them, and most are programmed to
pay out between 83 and 98 per cent.
But no matter how long you play,
unless you hit the jackpot, the amount
you win back will be a very small frac-
tion of the amount you bet.

What are your chances of hitting a
jackpot? In the three years before this
book was published, out of about 100
million visitors to Las Vegas, only five
people won jackpots of $100,000 or
more, and an additional four people
won jackpots over $1 million. It's the

possibility, however slight, of winning
a fortune that keeps people feeding all
those "one-armed bandits." Caesars
Palace encourages such notions by
reminding patrons that they have paid
out more million-dollar-plus jackpots
than any other casino in the world. Of
course, it has been operating for more
than 40 years as one of the city's largest
casinos, so this fact has nothing to do
with your chances of hitting it big.

How to Play

The slot machines in Caesars Palace
accept bets in denominations from one
penny to $500. The high-priced mac-
hines are located in separate, semiprivate
VIP areas. Many let you bet various
amounts on the same machine. Try it.
Find a quarter machine and feed a $10
bill into it. Pull the handle (or push the
button – it makes no difference). A
computer chip instantly picks a series
of random numbers, then makes the
whirling drums stop on the symbols
corresponding to those numbers. Cer-

Learning to Win

If you long to know
more about the art of
gambling, venture out
and pick up some
poolside reading at
Gamblers Book Shop
(630 South 11th
Street, tel: 702-382-
7555), the world's
largest bookshop
devoted entirely to
gambling and sports
betting books. Here
you'll find just about
every book in print
about casino gaming,
card and betting
strategies, income tax
avoidance tips, and
every other gambling-
related subject you
can imagine.

Food and Drink 🍴

① AUGUSTUS CAFE

Caesars Palace, 3570 Las Vegas
Boulevard South; tel: 702-731-7845;
daily 24hr; $–$$

Located by the front desk, this
casual coffee shop looks out on
Caesars Palace's Roman Plaza, with
its amphitheater used for parties and
receptions and its curious Brahma
Shrine, an exact replica of one of
Thailand's most popular Buddhist
shrines. Breakfast fare tends toward
the unusual, with such dishes as
carne asada scrambled eggs, and
almond-crusted French toast.

tain combinations mean you win. Nothing you can do, and nothing the machine has done before, will affect the outcome of the pull. Try it 39 more times, and you will have gambled the whole $10 bill once. Then cash out. (If you don't, the machine will let you keep going until you've lost all your credits.) Take the ticket the slot machine prints out to a cashier machine, which reads its bar code and gives you your money. Less than $10? Now you understand slot machines.

VIDEO POKER MACHINES

These, like other slot machines, work from a computer chip that generates random numbers and is programmed for a preset payout percentage. Instead of offering pie-in-the-sky jackpots, they pay smaller amounts more frequently, and you can improve your odds through careful analysis. This doesn't mean you're any more likely to walk away a winner, but it does mean that if your real purpose is to keep the waitress bringing free drinks, you can study the screen endlessly and play very slowly. If you need to brush up on your knowledge of poker hands – does a flush beat a straight? – video poker is the place to do it before moving up to other poker-based games like Caribbean stud or Pai Gow poker.

CRAPS

At most casino resorts, you can watch how-to-gamble lessons in your room on closed-circuit TV any hour of the day or

night, but they are no substitute for the actual experience of gambling on the casino floor. About two dozen resorts offer free table game lessons during the day, when the casino is not crowded. Caesars Palace offers lessons in five games at different times throughout the day (including at 11am, which fits in well with this tour; a second craps lesson at Caesars is daily at 5pm).

The Odds

The polar opposite of slot machine gambling, craps offers players the best odds of any casino game. It is also the most physical and extroverted, so many people are timid about trying it. The basic game is simple and depends entirely on chance. The betting layout is complicated, but you don't have to master it all. Most of the more complicated bets are "sucker bets," anyway. All you need to do is place your bet on the long, curved "pass line." In fact, you don't even have to know the rules – the dealer will either take your chip or give you another chip – but it's more fun if you understand the game.

When the person whose turn it is to shoot rolls the dice, if they come up 7 or 11 on first roll, you win, and if they come up 2, 3, or 12, you lose. If any other number comes up, it becomes the "point" that the shooter must roll again to win, before he rolls a 7 and loses ("craps out"). When a shooter loses, the dice are passed around the table to the next shooter. They will eventually come around to you, but if you don't want to be a shooter, you can pass them along to the next person.

Above: building up to a number six.

Caesar Salads
Around 336,000 Caesar salads are consumed in the restaurants at Caesars Palace every year. The salad is believed to hail from the 1924 recipe by chef Caesar Cardini, an Italian immigrant to the US.

ROULETTE

Roulette is the simplest of the casino's table games, which is why the free lesson (at noon) only takes 15 minutes. You can bet on one or more individual numbers, on clusters of numbers, or on whether the winning number will be even or odd, red or black. The dealer spins the roulette wheel, and whichever number the ball lands on wins. Because there are two extra numbers – "0" and "00" – the odds favor the house by about 5.3 per cent. Roulette tends to appeal to people who believe in the intrinsic power of numbers or their own precognition.

BLACKJACK

Next up is blackjack, by far the most popular table game in Las Vegas casinos; more people play blackjack than all other table games combined. Caesars Palace offers free blackjack lesson daily at 12:15pm and 3:15pm.

How to Play

The rules are deceptively simple. You play against the dealer, placing your bet before the cards are dealt, and whichever gets the card total closest to 21 without going over that number wins, double or nothing. The house advantage comes from the fact that

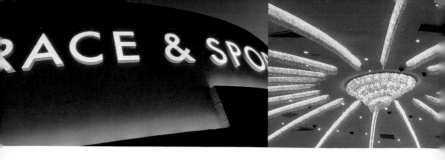

Headline Sports

Caesars Palace is known for its high-profile sporting events, something for which Las Vegas is world-renowned – especially for boxing. Heavyweight champion Joe Louis became a casino "greeter" at Caesars Palace after his long, illustrious boxing career ended.

Below: playing the slots at Caesars Palace.

one of the dealer's cards remains hidden until after you've decided whether to "hit" (take another card) or "stand." Rules about "doubling down" and "splitting pairs" let you raise the stakes on certain hands.

A beginner can play blackjack after a few minutes of instruction; to play the game well takes practice in analyzing your chances based on the card the dealer is showing. Betting strategy is everything, and blackjack play can produce what seem to be phenomenal runs of luck, good or bad.

Now's the time, perhaps, to reflect on what you have learned so far over lunch at **Bertolini's**, ①②. (Note that even the fanciest restaurants in Vegas can speed you through, if required, so it will still be possible to fit a decent lunch in, despite the busy schedule of gaming lessons in this tour.)

RACE AND SPORTS BOOK

Next to the People Mover pedestrian entrance, near the Colosseum concert hall and the Elton John gift shop, you'll find the two gaming areas where skill counts more than luck.

The race and sports book in Caesars Palace is one of the biggest and most spectacular in Las Vegas. Dimly lit, it has seating for 250 with seven big-screen television monitors – two of them 20 x 30ft (6m x 9m) in size. Smaller screens show all the major sporting events going on at the moment, and some seats have small plasma screens for watching horse races. A big electronic betting board displays the current odds on every pro sporting event coming up. You can bet on boxing, American football, basketball, baseball, golf, and hockey, auto racing, and horse racing. The rules for betting are different for various sports. Minimum bets are $10 for sports, $2 for races. Betting is not complicated, but information overload can be extreme. If you're not a seasoned sports betting buff, you might at least place a $10 bet on your team of choice.

Food and Drink 🍴

② BERTOLINI'S

Caesars Palace – Forum Shops, 3570 Las Vegas Boulevard South; tel: 702-735-4663; daily 11am–midnight; $$

This upscale Italian-style trattoria offers delicious Italian entrées and wood-oven pizza. Most patrons choose to dine "outdoors" near a huge and loud fountain.

POKER

Through a hallway from the race and sports book, the poker room has 30 tables. Few will be in use in the middle of the day, though when night falls they will all be packed. Poker is the only Las Vegas casino game where gamblers play against each other, not the house. Besides the familiar five-card draw, favorite games include Seven-card Stud, Omaha, and Texas Hold 'em; the last is by far the most popular live game in Vegas, and there are many tables at which this is the only game. At other tables games tend to alternate between the other different poker games. (As some cards in Texas Hold'em are shared by all the players, it is hard to deal this and other games at the same table.)

Most poker tables have limits on how much you can bet or raise. Many professional poker players live in Las Vegas, and more fly into town every weekend. High-limit and no-limit tables are intended to attract pro play, leaving low-limit tables safer for casual players. If you play poker well and often back home, the poker room offers a chance to pit your skills against a table full of strangers and find out how good you really are. If you are a beginner, it might be safer to practise on the video poker games and watch the in-room television poker lessons first.

Pai Gow Poker

Originally invented in the private poker clubs of California in the 1980s, Pai Gow poker is a hybrid version of pai gow, an ancient Chinese game played with domino-like tiles. (Caesars Palace is one of the casinos that also offers Pai Gow tables.) The poker version uses cards instead of tiles and poker hands instead of the original Chinese scoring combinations. You get seven cards, which you divide into a five-card hand and a two-card hand. If both your hands beat the dealer's two hands, you win, and if both the dealer's beat yours, you lose. If you beat the dealer on one hand and they beat you on the other, it's a "push" (tie), and you

Above from far left: test your luck with sporting events; even the lighting at Caesars is glitzy; no cheating, with a fresh pack of cards; a winning hand?

Poker Ploys

Regardless of status, motive, or method, most people make unconscious revelations through body language. In poker, this can be the difference between winning or losing. Tics, twitches, nervous laughs, or facial expressions can be crucial giveaways. Having a "tell" can be a disadvantage and overcoming it is as difficult as changing any other unconscous personal habit: someone might be too quick to flip their cards if they have a good hand, or slump in their seat if they do not. Pay attention to the body language of your opponents and you might walk away with more money in your pocket than if you don't. A tip from one professional poker player is this: sit down at the table and spot the sucker. If you haven't made them within five minutes, get up and leave. Otherwise, the sucker is you.

Above: enough to make your eyes spin.

Early Slots

Before slot machines were programmed with computer chips or spoke in digital voices urging you to play, coin-clattering mechanical "one-armed bandits" were standard fixtures in casinos for a hundred years. You can learn about slot machine heritage and, if you live in a state where private possession of slot machines is legal, buy one and ship it home at Showcase Slots and Antiquities (4305 South Industrial Road, tel: 702-740-5722, www. showcaseslots.com).

keep your bet. Due to the large number of pushes, Pai Gow poker is a relatively slow-paced game, and you can play for hours without losing or winning huge sums. Try to catch the 2pm lesson.

MINI-BACCARAT

Baccarat, which dates back to the 15th century, is the favorite casino game in Monte Carlo and many other parts of Europe. Its popularity spread to America as part of the James Bond mystique, and today at most large Las Vegas Strip casinos "big table" baccarat is played in a special roped-off area or separate room where Arab sheikhs and Asian business tycoons bet astonishing sums on the turn of a card. Mini-baccarat is the same game, but it is played

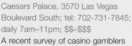

Food and Drink ③ CAFÉ LAGO BUFFET

Caesars Palace, 3570 Las Vegas Boulevard South; tel: 702-731-7845; daily 7am–11pm; $$–$$$

A recent survey of casino gamblers shows that they overwhelmingly prefer to eat at buffets rather than at the traditional restaurants non-gambling visitors choose. The Café Lago Buffet has seating areas indoors, in richly upholstered, U-shaped, high-backed booths, as well as outside on a terrace overlooking the pool area. Except for its setting, most locals would not rate the Café Lago as the best buffet in town, but with six cooking stations it does offer a broad enough selection to make "all you can eat" a real challenge. The spread includes salmon, crab, shrimp, prime rib, and an impressive array of Asian dishes.

at a smaller table on the main casino floor. The betting limits are lower, and you don't have to dress up.

Mini-baccarat, just like baccarat, is entirely a game of luck. A single player competes against a banker to see whose hand comes closest to "9" (face cards count "0," aces count "1"). Everybody else at the table simply bets on whether the banker or the player will win the hand. Bets pay 2 to 1; you can also bet that the two hands will tie, which pays 9 to 1. In mini-baccarat, the dealer turns over both the banker's and the player's hands. Betting strategies are similar to blackjack, but playing skill is not a factor in baccarat as it is in blackjack. A Mini-Baccarat lesson can be had at 4pm.

GARDEN OF THE GODS

If you are staying at Caesars Palace, and your head is reeling after a full day of learning about casino games, it's time to head for the pool for a little sunshine and relaxation. The exquisite 4.5-acre (2-hectare) **Garden of the Gods** swimming pool complex (Apr–Oct: daily, 8am–8pm, Nov–Mar: daily, 8am–6pm) is one of the best reasons to pick Caesars Palace as your hotel, since it is strictly for guests only. Lush gardens, tall palm trees, urns, statuary, and Roman columns of Carrara marble surround four pools, one of which is designated for topless bathing, and two large whirlpool baths. The complex is said to be modeled on the ancient Roman baths of Caracalla, and has mosaics inspired by those at Pompeii.

DINNER AND GAMBLING

If you want to stay longer at Caesars Palace, consider dining at the **Café Lago Buffet**, see ⑪③. Afterwards it is time to put your luck and learning to the test. Pick the action that appeals most to you and find a table that has an open seat, being careful to avoid the ones with high betting limits.

Place some cash on the table, and the dealer will push it down a slot and give you chips in return. Although casinos will not honor each other's chips, all use the same color coding system: red = $5, green = $25, black = $100. The dealer cannot redeem your chips or give change. At the end of the night, you have to go to one of the cashiers' cages to convert the chips back into cash.

Remember, the odds always favor the house, so the law of probabilities guarantees that you will always lose if you play long enough. The secret to winning is to quit while you're ahead, which can be very hard to do. Many serious gamblers will limit their time at the tables to short intervals and take any sizable win as a cue to quit playing. Others will bet their whole stake on one turn of the card or spin of the roulette wheel, knowing that the likelihood of doubling their money is greater than if they spread smaller bets over a longer time.

People who gamble while their judgment is impaired by alcohol tend to lose much more. Notice the waitresses dressed in togas who circulate through the casino offering players free drinks? That's why. Good luck…

Above from far left: lucky balls; wait staff are on hand to serve drinks as you gamble; casino currency; there is little more intimidating than the high-limit lounge.

Below: the Garden of the Gods, Caesars Palace.

BUDGET LAS VEGAS

To find fun on the cheap – or even for free – in a place where money reigns supreme might seem a real challenge. However, in the hope of taking more from you than you are expecting to spend, the city has lots of bargains.

Below: this tour's starting point – the Sahara – should be easy to spot

DISTANCE 4–5 miles (6–8km), for the daytime tour; 3–9 miles (5–14km) in the evening
TIME A full day
START Sahara
END Fremont Street
POINTS TO NOTE
Leave early. The double-decker Deuce bus ($2 a ride, $5 all-day pass) runs along the Strip and north to the Downtown Transit Center (300 North Casino Center Boulevard, tel: 702-228-7433) every 6 to 15 minutes round the clock.

Let's face it. Las Vegas is a bad place to be broke. Both the police and the resorts are notoriously intolerant of vagrants. For those who have lost all their money, the only realistic choice is to leave. But if you're a backpacker exploring America on a few dollars a day, or want to keep your spending for the casinos, the city does offer a lot to see and do on the cheap.

THE STRIP BY BUS

Start early (at around 8am) and catch the double-decker Deuce bus up or down the Strip, depending on where you're staying. When you board, buy a $5 all-day pass. Get off at the **Sahara** ❶ (2535 Las Vegas Boulevard South; tel: 702-737-2111 or 888-696-2121; www.saharavegas.com; *see pp.54 and 110*), which is at the far north end of the Strip, amid the ghosts of hotels past that have been razed to make way for future condominium towers and resort complexes. Unless you have already eaten, get off the bus for breakfast at the **Sahara Buffet**, see ⑪①.

SLOTS A FUN

Walk or bus from the Sahara south to this small casino next to Circus Circus. At **Slots A Fun** ❷ (2800 Las Vegas

Boulevard South; tel: 702-734-0410) you can gamble almost for free. About half the slot machines take pennies or nickels. There is also nickel video poker, as well as $1 blackjack tables. Instead of free drinks, the casino offers donuts to players in the morning and little sandwiches throughout the day.

STRIP ATTRACTIONS

Continue strolling up the Strip from one air-conditioned resort lobby to the next. There are numerous free attractions along the way, many of them described elsewhere in this book.

Circus Circus to the Venetian
On your right as you head up the Strip from Slots A Fun is **Circus Circus** ❸

Food and Drink 🍴
① SAHARA BUFFET
The Sahara, 2535 Las Vegas Boulevard South; tel: 702-737-2111; daily 7am–10pm; $–$$
Located on the second floor of the casino, this is the lowest-priced buffet on the Strip – you're sure to recognize it by the long line of expectant diners. Of all the meals, breakfast (which they stop serving at 10:30am) is the cheapest, costing just $8.99 for all you can eat. Fresh fruit, blintzes, waffles, meats, biscuits and gravy, mini-pastries, and design-your-own omelets, along with assorted Mexican breakfast items make this a great place to fill up with food and coffee for the day. If you're subtle about it, you can get away with putting some of the less gooey items, such as bacon and thumb-sized chocolate éclairs, in a plastic bag to take away for later.

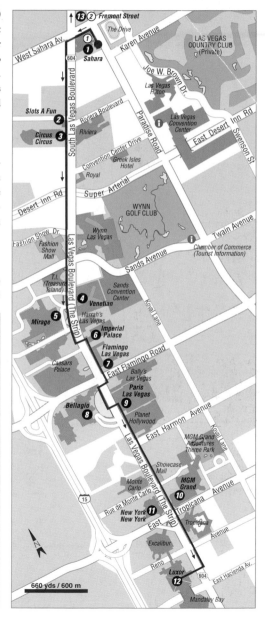

(2880 Las Vegas Boulevard South tel: 702-734-0410; *see pp.48 and 110*). Free attractions here include its extraordinary circus acts that take place above the casino floor.

Next, five blocks up on the left, is the **Venetian ❹** (3355 Las Vegas Boulevard South; tel: 702-414-1000; *see pp.36, 50, and 111*). Free highlights here include the Grand Canal and St. Mark's Square.

Mirage to the Flamingo

Opposite the Venetian, on your right, is the **Mirage ❺** (3400 Las Vegas Boulevard South; tel: 702-791-7111; *see also pp.32, 44, and 110*), heralding the start of the southern stretch of the Strip. Without spending a dime here, you can marvel at the Siegfried and Roy Plaza, the white tigers, the lobby aquarium, and the tropical rainforest.

Now continue past **Caesars Palace**, which is located next to the Mirage, and cross over to the **Imperial Palace ❻** (3535 Las Vegas Boulevard South; tel: 702-731-3311; *see p.43*). Here, you can visit the auto museum, which has free admission.

Adjacent to the Imperial Palace is the **Flamingo ❼** (3555 Las Vegas Boulevard South; tel: 702-733-3111; *see also pp.30, 34, and 112*). Stop by here to see the flamingo habitat.

Bellagio and Paris Las Vegas

One block farther on and on the other side of the road is **Bellagio ❽** (3600 Las Vegas Boulevard South; tel: 702-731-7110; *see pp.40, 45, and 112*). Time your walk so that you are at the lake in front of this hotel at 3pm, when the Strip's most spectacular free show starring the Bellagio's spectacular, choreographed fountains takes place in the lake in front of this hotel. It then continues on the half-hour until dusk (it runs every 15 minutes after dark). Next door, the volcano at the Mirage erupts in the evening only. Both of these sights are spectacular at night, if you want to return on another occasion.

After you have admired the fountain show, head inside to see the conservatory and botanical gardens, again all at no cost.

Cross over the Strip again to reach **Paris Las Vegas ❾** (3655 Las Vegas Boulevard South; tel: 702-740-6969; *see pp.43 and 114*). Here, the architecture and decor are the highlights.

MGM Grand to the Luxor

On the same side of the road, just one block down, is the **MGM Grand ❿** (3788 Las Vegas Boulevard South; tel: 702-891-1111; *see pp.35, 50, and 115*), where the lion habitat has no entrance fee. Opposite is **New York New York ⓫** (3790 Las Vegas Boulevard South;

Food and Drink 🍴

② SAN FRANCISCO SHRIMP BAR AND DELI
Golden Gate Hotel, 1 Fremont Street; tel: 702-385-1906; $
The Golden Gate Hotel started serving 50-cent shrimp cocktails in 1959. Half a century and 25 million shrimp cocktails later, the price has risen to 99 cents – still the best dining bargain in Las Vegas. The Hotel serves two tons of shrimp a week.

tel: 702-794-8200; *see also pp.46, 71, and 115*), remarkable for its architecture. The 47-story behemoth is Nevada's tallest casino at 529ft (160m) and its exterior of multiple façades is one of the Strip's most visually exciting.

Finally, you reach the **Luxor ⑫** (3900 Las Vegas Boulevard South; tel: 702-262-4000; *see also pp.46 and 113*), where attractions include the inclined elevators (though note that these can only be ridden by guests) in the atrium, which is said to be spacious enough to accommodate nine Boeing 747s.

DOWNTOWN

From the southern end of the Strip, take the Deuce double-decker bus all the way to Downtown *(see p.28)*. The bus makes frequent stops along the way. Our recommendation for dinner

is the **San Francisco Shrimp Bar and Deli**, see ⑪②, on **Fremont Street ⑬**.

Fremont Street Experience

Stay in Fremont Street for the centerpiece of Downtown's **Fremont Street Experience: Viva Vision** (nightly on the hour 8pm–midnight; free). This spectacular sound and light show is projected onto the world's largest LED screen, a vaulted canopy that covers four blocks of pedestrians-only Fremont Street and has a 550,000-watt sound system. There are more than a dozen shows, and no show is presented twice in the same night. They range from *Lucky Vegas*, featuring classic Vegas icons, and *Speed, Smoke, and Spinning Wheels*, with an auto racing theme, to the extraterrestrial *Area 51*, the psychedelic *The Drop*, and the sexy, adult-oriented, late-evening *Fahrenheit at Night*.

Above from far left: palm trees at the Flamingo; see the dolphins *(left)* and lions *(right)* for free at the Mirage; Eiffel Tower at Paris Las Vegas.

Free Acts
In earlier times, most Strip casinos had lounges where live singers and comedians performed without cover charge. Today, free lounge acts are less common, but they can still be found in a number of resorts on the Strip, including the Casbar Lounge in the Sahara; Margaritaville at the Flamingo; the Terrazza Lounge at Caesars Palace; the Indigo Lounge at Bally's; the Ava Lounge in the Mirage; and the Island Lounge at Mandalay Bay.

Left: New York New York has one of the most impressive façades in Vegas.

LAKE MEAD AND THE VALLEY OF FIRE

Don't get so caught up in Las Vegas that you overlook what its vicinity has to offer. Leave the themed tours behind and discover dramatic desert landscapes, ancient Indian art, and the largest man-made lake in the US.

The Environment

In earlier times, Lake Mead was seen as an almost unlimited water supply because all water used would otherwise be lost to evaporation. But as the water was diverted to supply California and Arizona, the water level has begun to fall so much that towns consumed in the lake's creation have re-emerged.

Below: teeming lake.

DISTANCE 134 miles (215km)
TIME Around 5 hours
START/END Las Vegas Strip
POINTS TO NOTE

This route is done by car and the mileage is heavy, so make sure you have a full gas tank. We do not recommend restaurants on this route, as you will be heading through barren terrain; ensure you bring drinking water plus snacks for the journey and sensible footwear. Aim to leave by 6:30am if you want to escape the heat of the day in summer.

Few Las Vegas visitors take time to explore the desert wonderland that lies just a few miles away on the other side of Sunrise Mountain. It's a shame, because this natural, pristine landscape presents the perfect counterpoint to the traffic-clogged, over-the-top, artificial environment of the Strip. This open-road trip will add a new dimension to your Vegas vacation.

LAS VEGAS TO LAKE MEAD

In the summer months, you will want to start out as early as possible. From the Strip, take Tropicana Avenue east to Paradise Road and turn right. As you pass the airport, Paradise will merge into Interstate 215 and take you to **Henderson ❶**, 12 miles (19km) from the Strip.

Beyond Henderson

The freeway ends at Henderson and becomes Lake Mead Drive. Continue for 10 miles (16km), past the Lake Las Vegas resort complex, to the **Lake Mead National Recreation Area ❷** entrance gate, where you pay a small charge per car, which discourages joyriding by local teenagers and, except on weekends, usually means you'll have

the road all to yourself. (If you pass through the gate before the fee station is open, pay at the self-service kiosk.) Just past the entrance, turn left onto Northshore Road.

NORTHSHORE ROAD

This scenic drive parallels the Lake Mead shoreline at a distance of about four miles (6km). For about half the way, the Black Mountains block your view of the lake, but the desert, with its other-worldly landscapes of bare rock in hues of red, white, black, and tan thinly scattered with ocotillo, creosote, and datura plants, provides plenty for the eyes to feast on. Several roads turn off to the right, providing access to the lakeshore, including paved roads to the Callville Bay and Echo Bay marinas.

Hiking Trails

Along the way are trailheads for two half-a-mile (1km) trails, the Northshore Summit and Redstone Dune hiking trails. Another beautiful stop along this leg of the trip is **Rogers Warm Spring** ❸, a palm-fringed oasis with a crystal-clear pool teeming with small fish.

VALLEY OF FIRE STATE PARK

It's 46 miles (74km) and approximately a 90-minute drive (more if you stop en route) from the Henderson entrance gate to the **Valley of Fire State Park** ❹ (tel: 702-397-2088; www.parks.nv.gov.vf.htm; park: daily 24 hrs; visitor center daily: 8:30am–

4:30pm; charge). Nevada's oldest and largest state park encompasses an ancient red-and-white sandstone formation, uplifted and fractured by faults over the eons to form rock labyrinths and strangely eroded formations. Some of the cliffs are decorated with elaborate petroglyphs carved by nomadic American Indians as much as 4,000 years ago. One of the best examples is high on the side of **Atlatl Rock**, reached by climbing a stairway from a picnic area on the scenic drive through the park.

For hikers, there is the fascinating half-mile (1km) trek to **Mouse's Tank**, said to have been the hideout of a legendary renegade Indian. Many species of birds and reptiles find shelter in the park, along with coyotes, foxes, skunks, tortoises, and jack rabbits. Hiking here is best done in the early morning, since it can be dangerously hot in the middle

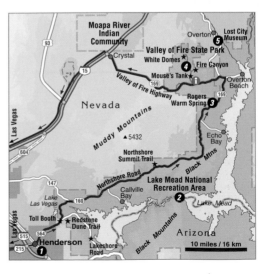

Above from left:
taking a dip in Lake Mead; Hoover Dam.

Lake Mead by Boat

The eastern shore of Lake Mead is not accessible by road, and most of the Colorado River arm of the lake cannot even be seen from any road. To explore the lake's hidden canyons, beaches, and inlets you need a boat. Houseboats, as well as water skiing and fishing boats and personal water craft, are available for rent at Callville Bay Marina (tel: 800-255-5561), 15 miles (24km) from the Henderson entrance station on a side road off Northshore Road, and at Echo Bay Marina (tel: 800-752-9669), 35 miles (56km) from the Henderson entrance. Reserve houseboats as far in advance as possible.

of the day. If you're one of the first hikers of the day in the sand-floored canyons, you will see the tracks left by hundreds of animals during the night.

LOST CITY MUSEUM

Located 8 miles (13km) north of the entrance to Valley of Fire along State Highway 169, the **Lost City Museum** ❺ (tel: 702-397-2193; www.comnett. net/kolson; daily 8:30am–4:30pm; charge) preserves ruins and artifacts from Pueblo Grande de Nevada, the largest ancient Indian archaeological site in the state, which was built by ancestral Pueblo people around A.D. 750 and thrived for four centuries before it was mysteriously abandoned. When its original location was about to be flooded by the creation of Lake Mead in the 1930s, the pueblo was taken apart, moved piece by piece, and reassembled

at its present site in the improbably green farming town of Overton.

RETURN TO LAS VEGAS

The shortest route back to Vegas involves returning south from Overton to the Valley of Fire and driving through the park along Highway 169, which cuts an almost straight path for 25 miles (40km) across empty, eroded terrain to join Interstate 15 at the corner of the Moapa Indian Reservation. This is the homeland of a small band of Paiutes, some of whom you may meet at the truck plaza near the Interstate 15 on-ramp.

From there, it is a fast 33-mile (53-km) trip back to town. The return trip from Valley of Fire takes about an hour. Aim to head back to the city by late morning, before the day gets unbearably hot.

Right: Lake Mead from above.

HOOVER DAM AND GRAND CANYON WEST

Two of the most spectacular man-made wonders of the American South-west (not counting Las Vegas itself), which were built 70 years apart, are found to the south-east of the city and can easily be visited in a single day.

Completed in 1936 after five years of construction at a cost of $49 million and 104 workers' lives, Boulder Dam (now known as Hoover Dam) was the most ambitious public works project of the Great Depression era. Spanning Black Canyon below the confluence of the Colorado and Virgin rivers, it created the largest man-made lake in the US that measures 110 miles (177km) long and some 500ft (152m) deep. After touring the dam, you can continue south to another, less utilitarian but equally dramatic, engineering feat built by the Hualapai Indians, which allows you to walk off the edge of the Grand Canyon.

> **DISTANCE** 246 miles (396km)
> **TIME** A full day
> **START/END** Las Vegas Strip
> **POINTS TO NOTE**
> This route is done by car and the mileage is heavy, so make sure you have a full gas tank. We do not recommend restaurants on this route, as you will be heading through barren terrain; ensure you bring drinking water plus snacks for the journey. Aim to leave fairly early (around 8:30am).

LAS VEGAS TO THE HOOVER DAM

After a bright-and-early breakfast, leave Las Vegas following the same route described in the previous route through Henderson to the Lake Mead National Recreation Area entrance gate *(see p.90)*. This time, continue straight after passing the gate to follow the Lakeshore Scenic Drive for 11 miles (18km), past Boulder Beach – a popular place to beat the heat on summer weekends – and the Las Vegas

Boat Harbor. The road climbs up to join US Highway 93 just east of Boulder City. Then you begin a 3-mile (5km) switchback descent into Black Canyon to arrive at Hoover Dam.

HOOVER DAM

Rising 726ft (221m) above the canyon floor, **Hoover Dam ❶** generates electricity for Los Angeles. The lake also supplies water to the cities of Anaheim and San Diego, California – but not Las Vegas. The conspicuous consumption of electrical power and water on the Las Vegas Strip was originally conceived in the belief that the city would

Below: a wave from the Hoover Dam; take care in the heat.

have unlimited resources from the dam, but while the populations of both Las Vegas and Southern California grew, no such water or power was available to Las Vegas. Today, the Strip's electricity comes from a coal-fired power plant located to the north of the city, while its water comes from wells, as municipal government fights with farmers and ranchers in outlying areas for the right to pump more water from the ground.

Hoover Dam Visitors' Center

After paying the admission fee to the **Hoover Dam Visitors' Center**, you can sign up for a tour that takes you into the depths of the dam's interior for a close-up look at the huge generators and spillway. For free, you can walk on the sidewalk along the top of the dam, and stare down at the curved expanse of concrete that fills the canyon below, and admire the

strangely symbolic Art Deco statues and mosaics. Because of security concerns since the 9/11 terrorist attacks, day packs, large purses, and similar-size bags are not allowed on or inside the dam.

GRAND CANYON WEST

As you drive across Hoover Dam, you enter the state of Arizona. Notice the clocks on each end of the dam. In the winter months, it is one hour later in Arizona, which is on Mountain Time, than in Nevada, which is on Pacific Time. But since Arizona does not observe Daylight Saving Time, during the summer months the time is the same on both sides of the dam.

Continue south for 42 miles (68km) on US Highway 93 to the turnoff on the left marked with a large billboard for **Grand Canyon West ❷**. Follow Pearce Ferry Road for 30 miles (48km)

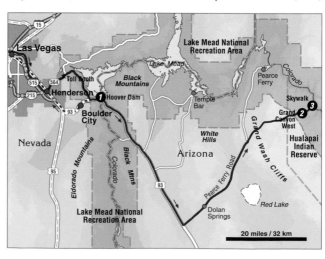

to a well-marked Y-junction, where the right fork – Diamond Bar Road – goes another 15 miles (24km) to Grand Canyon West.

Attractions

Owned by the Hualapai Indian Tribe, whose reservation spans more than 100 miles (160km) of the Grand Canyon Rim, this recreation area will probably have a resort hotel and Indian casino some day. But for now, its attractions include a petting zoo, wagon rides, Indian cultural performances at **Hualapai Ranch**, a hiking trail to a scenic canyon overlook at Guano Point, site of a historic, long-abandoned bat manure mine, and Grand Canyon West's premier attraction, the Skywalk.

The Skywalk

A cantilevered, gulp-inducing glass walkway, the **Skywalk ❸** protrudes out from the canyon rim in a U-shape with no visible means of support, letting visitors stare straight down at the Colorado River some 4,000ft (1,219m) below. Although it feels frighteningly unsafe, engineering reports assure visitors that the bridge can support more than 71 million lb (32 million kg), withstand hurricane-force winds, and survive a magnitude 8.0 earthquake. Though the walkway is glass, it is supported by more than one million pounds of structural steel. On a first-come, first-served basis, 120 people are allowed on the Skywalk at one time. The admission charge has recently been lowered to $25 per person.

BACK TO LAS VEGAS

By now it will probably be around 2pm. Retrace your route from Grand Canyon West back over Hoover Dam. From there, you may wish to save time by driving back to the city via US Highway 93/95 instead of Lakeshore Drive. This route will take you back through **Boulder City**, a charming little all-American town built by the federal government to house dam construction workers away from the temptations of Las Vegas. Gambling is not allowed here. The entire return trip along this route should take about two hours, bringing you back to your hotel in plenty of time to rest up for dinner and a show.

Photo Opportunities
You are not allowed to carry cameras or other personal objects onto the Skywalk for fear that dropping them could scratch the glass or litter the canyon below, but you can photograph it from the rim and have a commercial photo taken of yourself on the bridge.

Below: braving the Skywalk.

DIRECTORY

A user-friendly alphabetical listing of practical information, plus hand-picked hotels and restaurants, clearly organised by area, to suit all budgets and tastes.

A–Z   98
ACCOMMODATIONS   110
RESTAURANTS   118

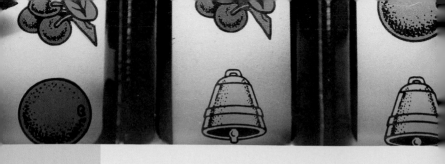

A-Z

A

AGE RESTRICTIONS

No-one under 21 is permitted in casinos, and minors under 18 years of age are not permitted on the Strip without a parent or guardian after 9pm on weekends and holidays. The state of Nevada does not permit anyone under the age of 21 to drink alcohol in public places, and you should keep some kind of picture identification, such as a passport or driving license, on your person, in case you are asked for proof of age.

B

BUDGETING

Credit and direct debit cards are accepted throughout Las Vegas. You'll find cash machines in most hotel lobbies. To avoid high surcharges levied on non-bank ATM machine transactions, consider getting cash back from purchases at a non-casino business. The days of rock-bottom deals in Las Vegas may be a thing of the past, but it's still possible to enjoy all-you-can-eat buffets, cheap (or even free) casino bar drinks, and midweek hotel package deals. Today, though, the sheer quality of the lodging and dining options, shows, and attractions is so tempting, a couple should consider budgeting at least $100/day, excluding accommodations, to take advantage of all Las Vegas has to offer – more if high-end dining and the most popular shows interest

you. Big conventions (a year-round phenomenon in Las Vegas) affect prices and cause hotel rooms and shows to sell out. Savvy travelers plan their trips around these, if possible.

C

CHILDREN

Child-friendly resorts, such as Circus Circus and Excalibur, often allow kids under 12 to stay for free in their parents' rooms, and have well-priced buffets that are ideal for families. Most hotels have pools, and many provide programs for children and teenagers, while babysitters and childcare facilities are also sometimes available.

Although Las Vegas remains primarily a gaming destination, families will have no difficulty finding activities suited to children on the Strip. In addition to the suggestions on our Las Vegas With Kids tour *(see pp.48–51)*, there's an Imax theater at the Luxor; bowling at Orleans and Green Valley Ranch; and a number of outdoor attractions, such as Valley of Fire State Park, Red Rock Canyon, Hoover Dam, and surrounding national parks that are tailor-made for youngsters. A car is recommended if you are visiting with children: walking distances are much greater than they appear, especially in hot desert sun.

Childcare

There are onsite childcare centers at all Coast Casinos and Station Casinos, including the Orleans, Green Valley

Ranch, South Coast, Sunset Station, Gold Coast, and Palace Station. Kids aged between 2 and 12 are welcome for a maximum of five hours daily from 9am to midnight (to 1am on Sat). The fee is around $6 per child per hour. Parents must remain on the premises.

The Hyatt Regency Lake Las Vegas Resort has a Camp Hyatt recreational program for kids aged 3 to 12. Cost per session is $27 to $40. Professional babysitting services are available: ask your hotel concierge for recommendations. There's usually a four-hour minimum of about $60 per child.

CLIMATE

Las Vegas is in the Mojave Desert and is hot and arid with extreme temperature ranges. The average rainfall is just over 4 inches (10.5cm) a year, and humidity is frequently below 10 per cent in summer. Average highs in summer top 100°F (38°C) daily with night-time lows of 71–81°F (22–27°C). Things start cooling down in November, with winter highs in the upper 50s°F (14°C) and lows in the upper 30s Fahrenheit (4°C), with higher precipitation and the occasional snowfall. The best time to visit is fall or spring, when daytime temperatures are balmy and nights are cool.

CLOTHING

In summer, pack light, casual, breathable clothing; a bathing suit; a broad-brimmed hat; sunglasses; neck protection; sunscreen with an SPF of 30 or above; and sturdy lightweight walking sandals or lace-ups for walking the long distances around hotel/casinos and museums, the Strip, Downtown, and excursions to surrounding outdoor attractions. Although shorts and T-shirts are the norm, those in the know bring long-sleeved shirts and pants (trousers) to protect exposed skin from strong sun in summer and fierce air conditioning inside buildings. Formal attire is rarely necessary: one dress-up outfit for women and a jacket for men are all you'll probably need. Between November and April, temperatures can get surprisingly chilly, so bring a sweater with you. Any time except summer wear layers and carry a waterproof jacket and a hat.

CRIME AND SAFETY

Visiting Las Vegas is safer than ever these days, with few violent crimes reported and very visible policing, private security guards, and surveillance cameras in public places, as well as VIVA Patrol volunteers trained by the police available to help out in tourist areas. Theft of personal property is quite common, however, so keep an eye on your belongings in busy areas, keep valuables locked in in-room safes, and buckets of coins in your lap, not next to slot machines in casinos.

CURRENCY AND TAXES

American dollars come in bills of $1, $5, $10, $20, $50, and $100. The dollar is divided into 100 cents. Coins come in

Do a Deal
Sin City is a place that likes to do deals, and car rental firms and even major casinos offer extremely low prices, usually in the hot summer months. Always bargain.

BIKINI
MIDNIGHT
PAYBACK ON SLOTS
BEER
GIRLS
BULL

Slot Machines
Casino owners never let an opportunity of getting their hands on your money slip by: there are slot machines for each denomination of coin.

1 cent (penny), 5 cents (nickel), 10 cents (dime), 25 cents (quarter), 50 cents (half-dollar), and $1 denominations.

There is no value-added tax (VAT) in the US, and Nevada does not charge state taxes. The city of Las Vegas does charge a local sales tax, however: 7.75 per cent on purchases and 9 per cent on hotel rooms (an extra 2 per cent tax is added to some rooms on or near the Fremont Street Experience). Car-rental companies charge both sales tax and service fees.

CUSTOMS

You can bring the following duty-free items into the US: 1 liter of alcohol (if over 21 years of age); 200 cigarettes, 50 cigars (not Cuban), or 2kg of tobacco, (if over 18 years of age); and gifts worth up to $100 ($800 for US citizens). Travelers with more than $10,000 in US or foreign currency, travelers' checks, or money orders must declare these upon entry. Meats, fruits, vegetables, seeds, or plants (and many prepared foods from them) are not permitted and must be disposed of in the bins provided before entering. For more information, contact US Customs & Border Protection (877-227-5511; www.cbp.gov).

D

DISABLED TRAVELLERS

Las Vegas attracts many seniors and has the largest number of ADA-accessible guest rooms in the nation.

Casinos are almost always on the ground floor, and hotel resorts typically have elevators and ramps in addition to stairs, making them easy to get around for visitors with reduced mobility. For more information, request the free *Access Las Vegas* brochure from the Las Vegas Convention and Visitors Authority's ADA Coordinator (702-892-0711; 800-326-8888; www.las vegas24hours.com).

E

ELECTRICITY

The US uses 110 to 120 volts AC (60 cycles). If visiting from outside North America, you may require an electrical adapter for any electronics or appliances you want to bring. Las Vegas electrical outlets accept the standard North American plug with two flat parallel pins.

EMBASSIES

Foreign embassies are all located in Washington, DC. Phone numbers include Britain (tel: 202-462-1340); Germany (tel: 202-298-4000); France (tel: 202-944-6000); and Australia (tel: 202-797-3000). Call directory enquiries (tel: 118) or check on www. directoryenquiries.org for the numbers of other embassies.

EMERGENCIES

In case of emergency, call 911. Dial 311 to report a non-emergency incident.

G

GAMBLING HELP

Some people gamble unwisely and get in over their heads, and for them help is just a phone call away. Sponsored jointly by the Nevada Resort Association and the Nevada Council on Problem Gambling, trained counselors stand by 24 hours a day at 800-522-4700, and all calls are confidential. Gamblers Anonymous, a nationwide program for gambling addicts similar to Alcoholics Anonymous, is also active in Las Vegas. There are meetings daily in and around Las Vegas. Their hotline number is 888-442-2110 or log on to www.gamblersanonymous.org.

GAMING ETIQUETTE

Players must be 21 years or over. No cell phones or electronics are allowed anywhere on the casino floor. Smoking is still permitted in casinos (but largely prohibited elsewhere in the city, *see p.105*).

GAY AND LESBIAN

The gay and lesbian scene is growing in conservative Las Vegas and GLBT travelers will find bars, clubs, drag shows, and the big Las Vegas Pride Parade in late May, and the Gay New Year's Eve Party. The Fruit Loop area, just 1 mile (2km) east of the Strip near the intersection of East Harmon Avenue and Paradise Road, is the closest thing the city has to a gay center.

For more information, pick up copies of the local publications *Bugle Q Vegas* (www.qvegas.com) or *Out Las Vegas* (www.outlasvegas.com) at one of the bars; Pride Factory (Suite E-1B, Commercial Center, 953 E. Sahara Ave; 702-444-1291; www.pridefactory.com), a gay gift shop and Internet Cafe open 10am–midnight; or at Get Booked, the local gay and lesbian community bookstore (4640 Paradise Rd., 702-737-7780; www.getbooked. com). The Gay and Lesbian Center (953 E. Sahara Avenue, Ste. B-25, Commercial Center; 702-733-9800) hosts gay and lesbian social groups and special events and has helpful information.

GUIDED TOURS

One of the beauties of Las Vegas is that it's an excellent jumping-off point for a remarkable variety of scenic attractions within a day's drive. Most tour operators aim their tours at short-term visitors interested in seeing attractions from the comfort of an air-conditioned bus, Jeep, helicopter, or light aircraft. But you can also find guided tours aimed at outdoors and history buffs, including bicycle tours, back-country Jeeping, whitewater rafting, and ghost towns.

Guided tours of Hoover Dam, Red Rock Canyon, Lake Mead, Death Valley National Park, the North Rim of Grand Canyon National Park, as well as Zion and Bryce National Parks are available through reputable tour operators such as Gray Line Bus Tours, Pink Jeep Tours, Papillon Helicopter Tours, Desert Eco Tours, Black

Above from far left: big, brash signs on the Strip and Downtown.

Disabled Parking If you rent a car, you should bring your hometown parking permit, or request a free 90-day permit through the city of Las Vegas at the Parking Permit Office, tel: 702-222-6431.

Canyon River Adventures, and Escape Adventures/Las Vegas Cyclery, to name a few. Pick-up is usually available at hotels on the Strip.

A handful of tour operators offer tours of Las Vegas itself. Gray Line Bus Tours (tel: 702-384-1234; 800-634-6579; www.grayline.com) has a nightly six-hour "Neon & Lights" tour, which combines bus ride and walking. A daytime tour takes in Clark County Museum, a history museum.

The 2.5-hour "Haunted Vegas Tour" (702-737-5540; www.hauntedvegas tour.com; 9pm Sat–Thur), based at the Greek Isles Hotel and Resort, combines a cheesy show and guided bus tour to sites such the Motel of Death (where several celebrities have been murdered) with tales about the restless shades of Bugsy Siegel, Liberace, Elvis, and others.

Vegas Walks (702-376-1054 or 800-313-6080; www.vegaswalks.com) does historical walking tours of the Strip with guides – a good way to get a handle on Las Vegas's dizzying changes over the last few decades.

Several companies also offer aerial views of Las Vegas. The most leisurely is probably Las Vegas Airship Tours (2642 Airport Drive, North Las Vegas; tel: 702-646-2888), which allows you to float gently above the Strip in a nine-passenger blimp. Also leisurely is Balloon Las Vegas (tel: 702-596-7582), which rounds off both its sunrise and sunset flights with a Champagne celebration.

H

HEALTH

Human beings were not designed to walk around in 100°F (38°C) midday temperatures; hang out in artificially cold, air-conditioned environments;

Right: slots at the Riviera.

remain seated almost motionless for hours at a time in a casino; eat large quantities of food at an all-you-can-eat buffet; or stay awake for 24 hours at a time. But then the Las Vegas Experience is not the everyday one. It's an extreme blowout of just a few days' duration, for most people. That's what makes it so much fun! In order to keep the fun coming, take the following general precautions, none of which should interfere with having a good time; it should, in fact, prolong it.

Wear a sunblock of 30SPF, sunglasses, a broad-brimmed hat, long- sleeved breathable clothing, and sturdy walking shoes when you walk around outside. Savvy desert residents (including native wildlife) are active outdoors in the early morning, before the sun gets too strong, and in the evenings, after the sun goes down. Your best bet is to stay inside between 2pm and 6pm, the hottest time of day in the desert, perhaps napping, pampering yourself, and/or visiting a museum, then stroll down the Strip and around Downtown for dinner, to catch a show, or see Las Vegas's amazing neon lights.

Keep a 1-liter water bottle with you (and keep sipping on it) at all times, to avoid dehydration, and snack on nutritious foods such as salty nuts to maintain an electrolyte balance in the body, especially if you're also drinking strong coffee and alcohol or taking medications, which are very dehydrating. Drinking too much water and eating too little food (hyponutremia) is an underreported danger in the desert, with serious health consequences.

Visitors with fair skin and light-colored eyes should be particularly alert for signs of heat exhaustion (red face, sweating, dizziness), which can come on quickly without your realizing it due to low humidity. Its more serious second stage, heat stroke (pale skin, dizziness, nausea, and lack of sweat), indicates a dangerous overheating of the body core and inability to cool down and should be treated medically, if suspected. To avoid problems, keep the skin and clothing wet (a wet bandana around the neck is an excellent idea) and keep the skin covered to maintain homeostatis in the body. Be careful around the pool. Plunging into cool water when your body has become overheated is inadvisable.

Medical Assistance

Walk-in medical clinics are much cheaper than hospital emergency rooms for minor ailments. Foreign visitors are strongly advised to purchase travel insurance before leaving to avoid high urgent-care costs.

University Medical Center (UMC) operates 11 Quick Care clinics in Las Vegas (www.umc-cares.org/quickcares). Two 24-hour medical services are available: (tel: 800-DOCS-911 and 702-735-3600). There is a medical clinic (tel: 702-309-5144, Mon–Fri, 8am–5pm) on the eighth floor of the Imperial Palace Hotel open to hotel guests. Nearby are the Summerlin Hospital Medical Center (tel: 702-283-7000), Boulder City Hospital (tel: 702-293-4111), and Lake Mead Hospital (tel: 702-649-7711).

Above from far left: gilded city: Downtown and on the Strip.

Birdwatching

What might sound like an unlikely stop is Henderson's Water Reclamation Facility (Moser Drive, near where Sunset intersects the Boulder Highway, tel: 702-566-2940, daily 6am–3pm), which has been designated as a Bird Viewing Preserve. A local branch of the Audubon Society has documented 200 different species here: early morning is the most rewarding time to visit.

HOURS AND HOLIDAYS

Las Vegas is a city that never sleeps, and casinos are open 24 hours, every day of the year, as are many service stores, supermarkets, and other businesses. Banks usually keep business hours of 9am to 3pm on weekdays and one evening until 6pm. Post offices are open 9am to 6pm weekdays and 8am to noon on Saturday.

Public Holidays

Public holidays include: New Year's Day (Jan 1); Martin Luther King Day (3rd Monday in Jan); Washington's Birthday (3rd Mon in Feb); Memorial Day (last Mon in May); Independence Day (July 4); Labor Day (1st Mon in Sept); Columbus Day (2nd Mon in Oct); Veterans' Day (Nov 11); Thanksgiving (4th Thur in Nov); and Christmas Day (Dec 25).

MEDIA

Las Vegas has two daily papers: the *Las Vegas Review Journal* and the *Las Vegas Sun*. *City Life* and *Las Vegas Weekly* are free alternative papers available at many locations. There are seven television stations and 30 radio stations. A traveler's newsletter, the *Las Vegas Advisor*, offers tips on getting the most out of your Las Vegas trip and is available by subscription from Huntingdon Press (800-244-2224).

What's On (www.ilovevegas.com), a free weekly in-room guide, is a good place to find information about hotel and tour packages. *Las Vegas Life* (www.lvlife.com), a monthly glossy magazine, has insider information on Las Vegas living.

Casino Player (www.casinoplayers.com) is a trade magazine aimed at serious gamers. For the latest insider information on what's happening in Las Vegas and how to get the most out of your trip, log on to www.lasvegasinsider.com, www.lasvegasadvisor.com, and www.cheapovegas.com.

OUTDOOR ACTIVITIES

It may seem unlikely but Las Vegas is actually a terrific base for day trips to numerous surrounding outdoor destinations, where you can hike, bike, horseback ride, camp, kayak, water ski, go whitewater rafting or speedboating, or just take in incredible desert scenery and history. Water sports such as water skiing, speed boating, and kayaking are popular on Lake Mead, south-east of Las Vegas.

The best hiking can be found amid the red rocks of Valley of Fire State Park, on the north end of Lake Mead NRA, and Red Rock Canyon National Conservation Area, 30 miles (48km) west of Las Vegas. Ten miles (16km) beyond Red Rock Canyon are the Spring Mountains, topped by lofty Mount Charleston, a good place to camp as well as hike and escape desert heat in summer and enjoy snow sports in winter.

Farther afield, Grand Canyon, Zion, Bryce Canyon, Joshua Tree, and Death Valley national parks are renowned for their extraordinary scenery and outdoor activities. Hoover Dam is a must-see for its historic importance as well as the sheer scope of its engineering.

POST

The Downtown post office is located at 201 Las Vegas Boulevard South, Ste. 100, and is open Monday to Friday 8:30am to 5pm. There is a post office just west of the Strip at 3100 South Industrial Road, open Monday to Friday 8:30am to 6pm, and 9am to 3pm on Saturdays. The post office at the airport is open Monday to Friday 9am to 1pm and 2pm to 5pm.

Effective first-class domestic postage rates are 41 cents for the first ounce (28g) with 17 cents for each additional ounce. Postcards are 24 cents each. Overseas postage is 84 cents for 1oz; 63 cents to Mexico and Canada. Postcards cost 75 cents to send; 55 cents to Canada and Mexico.

SMOKING

In keeping with the Sin City approach to life of "anything goes," smoking is very common in Las Vegas, especially on the casino floor. Smoking is not permitted in restaurants, bars serving food, at the airport, or the convention center. Hotels offer nonsmoking rooms, but if you are sensitive to cigarette smoke, choose one that is entirely non-smoking and patronize establishments with clear non-smoking policies.

TELEPHONES

The area code for Las Vegas is 702. Local calls are free (although some hotels impose an access charge for in-room calls). Calls from a coin box will require change, a credit card, or calling card available at many supermarkets. Some callboxes offer Internet access by the minute. For local information, dial 411. For toll-free 800 and 877 numbers, dial 1-800-555-1212.

TICKETS

The sheer number of show and concerts in Las Vegas is staggering. There's something here for everyone, from the Folies Bergère to lounge acts, the cerebral antics of the Blue Men, or concerts by headliners such as Elton John and Celine Dion. Tickets usually go on sale three months in advance for the most popular shows. For the best seats, call the day these go on sale – they sell out very fast – and expect to pay $100–$220 per person.

If an event is sold out, you may be able to get tickets (at super premium prices) through a reputable online broker such as www.tickco.com. Avoid buying tickets through eBay and other

Above from far left: a fabulous landscape outside Las Vegas that even super-wealthy Steve Wynn couldn't afford; flying over the Grand Canyon offers spectacular views.

Hit the Slopes
The Las Vegas Ski and Snowboard Resort is just 45 minutes away from Las Vegas by car and offers a different kind of exhilarating experience. Over 120in (305cm) of snow falls on the Spring Mountains, where it is located each year. Visit www.skilasvegas.com for details.

auction sites, as fraud is rife. High-rollers in the casinos are often given complimentary premium show tickets as an added incentive, so if you want Las Vegas at your feet, win big.

TIME DIFFERENCES

Most of Nevada is in the Pacific Time Zone; two hours behind Chicago, three hours behind New York, and eight hours behind London.

TIPPING

Plan on tipping 15–20 percent of the before-tax total on meals, and the same amount for taxi drivers and tour guides. Valets usually receive $2; housekeeping $2 per day; concierge services $5; and bell hops $1–2 per bag. A small bet for the dealer is the usual method of tipping at gaming tables. A small tip is also appropriate for keno runners and slot attendants.

TOURIST INFORMATION

The main one-stop shop for information is Las Vegas Convention and Visitors Authority (3150 Paradise Road (corner of Desert Inn Road); tel: 702-892-7575; toll free 1-877-847-4858; fax: 702-892-7553; www.lv24 hours.com), which has specialized information on everything from getting married to facilities for disabled travelers to visiting with kids.

LVCVA has tourist information offices abroad to help you plan your trip. On the web, look up www.lasvegas

freedom, plus the suffix for your country (www.lasvegasfreedom.co.uk, for the UK, for example). Other good sites include www.vegas.com for attractions, and www.lv chamber.com for events and local news. The State of Nevada Welcome Centers (www.travelnevada.com) also offer good information, if you're driving to Las Vegas.

There are Welcome Centers at Mesquite, near the Utah state line, and Primm, near the California state line.

TRANSPORTATION

Airports and Arrival

Most people fly or drive to Las Vegas or arrive by Greyhound bus. There is no longer any rail service to the city. Vegas is served by McCarran International Airport (tel: 702-261-5211; http://mccarran.com), 1 mile (2km) from the Strip and 5 miles (8km) from Downtown. One of the 12 busiest airports in the world, it has 1,100 flights daily via 40 different carriers and direct connections to 125 US cities. A record 46.2 million passengers passed through this airport in 2006. The most economical way to reach your hotel is by 24-hour shuttle; fares to the Strip and Downtown are less than $10. Taxi fares start at $2.70, with $1.80 per mile (2km) thereafter.

Car Rental

All the major rental car companies have kiosks at the airport; rates begin at $25–30 per day. You must be 21 or over (25 at some locations) to rent a car and have a valid driver's license and at least one major credit card. Air conditioning is vital, if you don't want to cook inside your vehicle. Dream Car Rentals (tel: 702-731-6452) and Rent-a-Vette (tel: 702-736-2592) specialize in exotic cars. Eaglerider (tel: 800-900-9901) rents motorcycles.

Las Vegas has wide boulevards, and getting around by car is easy. Parking isn't allowed on the Strip: use free valet parking at hotel casinos and then tip the valet a couple of bucks.

Driving

The main route through Las Vegas is Interstate 15 (I-15) from Los Angeles, California, a four-hour drive away, substantially longer when traffic is heavy on holiday weekends. I-15 continues north, through scenic Virgin River Gorge to Saint George, Utah, a good jumping-off point for national parks including Zion, Bryce, and the Grand Canyon. I-15 continues north to the state capital of Salt Lake City. If you're driving from Phoenix, Arizona, take Highway 93 north via I-40 and Hoover Dam to Las Vegas.

A word of caution: If you plan on driving through the desert, be sure to carry a good map, a spare tire, extra water – at least a gallon (4 liters) per person per day to avoid dehydration – nutritious snacks, and let someone know where you are going. A cellphone is a good idea but may not work in some areas; the same is true for GPS units powered by satellite.

Service stations may be few and far between outside Las Vegas; fill up when you can. If your car breaks down on a backroad, don't attempt to strike out on foot, even with water. A car is easier to spot than a person and provides shelter from the elements. Sit tight and wait to be found.

Public Transportation

Public bus transportation is operated by Citizens Area Transit (CAT). There are numerous bus routes throughout the area; a one-way fare on the Strip costs $2, and slightly less in the rest of the city. Buses on the Strip run 24 hours a day, seven days a week. For the latest information and scheduling, call CAT-RIDE (tel: 702-228-7433, www.rtcsouthernnevada.com). A trolley runs the length of the Strip 9:30 am to 1:30am. Reasonable fares and good-value day passes are available.

The privately funded Las Vegas Monorail (Mon–Thur 7am–2am, Fri–Sun 7am–3am) travels along the east side of the Strip behind the resorts, from the Sahara Hotel to the MGM Grand, with the following stops in between: Las Vegas Hilton, Las Vegas Convention Center, Harrah's/Imperial Palace, the Flamingo/Caesars Palace, and Bally's/Paris.

V

VISAS AND PASSPORTS

Foreign travelers to the US (including, as of January 2007, those from Canada and Mexico) must carry a valid passport and a visa is required for visits of more than 90 days. A return plane ticket is also normally required. Reg-

ulations are subject to change so for the most current information, contact the US Department of Homeland Security at www.dhs.gov.

W

WEBSITES AND INTERNET CAFES

Log on to the Las Vegas Convention and Visitors Authority website (www. visitlasvegas.com) to plan your trip. Other websites are noted in "Tourist Information" *(see p.106)*.

Foreign visitors should be aware that their laptop modem may not work in the US. Check that you have a global modem before you leave or buy a local PC-card modem when you arrive. For more information, log on to www. teleadapt.com.

Many, but not all, hotels in Las Vegas offer phones with dataports and local dial-up or high-speed Internet access. Increasingly, you will also find free wireless (Wi-Fi) Internet access in Vegas. Free Wi-Fi spots currently include McCarran Airport, Clark County Public Library, the Tropicana Hotel, and outside the Apple Store at Fashion Show Mall.

If you do not have a computer but want to check your email or surf the Internet, check out one of the local Internet Cafes. They include Pride Factory (Suite E-1B, Commercial Center, 953 East Sahara Avenue; tel702-444-1291; www.pridefactory. com; daily 10am–midnight); Elysium Internet Cafe (7875 West Sahara Avenue, #101; tel: 702-307-4931; daily 24 hours).

Although very expensive to use, there are branches of FedEx Kinko's between the Strip and the convention center (tel: 702-951-2400, daily 24 hours), near the UNLV campus (tel: 702-735-4402, daily 7am–midnight), and near Downtown (tel: 702-383-7022, daily 7am–11pm). They each have a T-Mobile Wi-Fi Hotspot.

WEDDINGS

With its easy-to-obtain marriage licenses and thousands of over-the-top nuptial options, Las Vegas is the wedding capital of the world. Neither blood tests nor waiting periods are required if you want to tie the knot. The legal age is 18 for both men and women (proof of age is required) and licensing fees are $55. Civil ceremonies can be performed at the Marriage Commissioner's Office at 309 South 3rd Street Chapel fees vary depending on the services provided. For marriage license information contact the Clark County Marriage License Bureau (201 Clark Avenue; located on the northwest corner of Clark Avenue and Third Street; tel: 702-671-0600; daily 8am–midnight, including holidays).

Same-sex marriages aren't recognized in Nevada but same-sex commitment ceremonies can be arranged through gay-owned Viva Las Vegas Villas & Wedding Chapel (800-574-4450; www.vivalasvegasweddings. com).

You can get married in Vegas even if you're not a US resident. To recognize

the union legally, most countries require a certified copy of your marriage certificate ($10) and an apostille from the Nevada Secretary of State ($20). Contact your home country's consulate office in Washington, DC, to inquire if additional certifications are required.

WEIGHTS AND MEASURES

Despite efforts to convert to metric, the US still uses the Imperial system of weights and measures. However, note that the US gallon is approximately 16 per cent smaller than the standard Imperial gallon.

WOMEN

Like New Orleans, Las Vegas is unabashedly a party town, where you are encouraged to act out on your fantasies, lubricated by large quantities of low-cost alcoholic drinks and a permissive attitude enshrined in Vegas's marketing theme. "What happens in Vegas, stays in Vegas." For women, this can be a mixed bag. In such an atmosphere, men are encouraged to view women as objects for their pleasure, and the old stereotype of the high-roller and his beautiful call girl is still very much a part of the scene, even though prostitution is officially illegal. If you're a solo woman, you'll find plenty of flirting in Las Vegas's burgeoning club scene – and perhaps some harassment by obnoxious drunken young men.

Greater Las Vegas is now home to an ever-growing stream of families, attracted to the pleasant residential communities, so you should have few problems away from the Strip. The level of policing in security-conscious Las Vegas should allow any woman to feel safe walking around, though. Just take the usual precautions with handbags and valuables.

Above from far left: glitzy casino sign; girly day out.

Below: vintage visitor.

ACCOMMODATIONS

Circus Circus Hotel, Theme Park, and Casino

2880 Las Vegas Boulevard South, tel: 702-734-0410 or 800-634-3450; www. circuscircus.com; $

The granddaddy of all themed resorts on the Strip, Circus Circus is gaudy fun and a good place for families to stretch their dollar (room specials run as low as $45 per night). Aside from Big Top performers, the Adventure-drome, and a carnival, the hotel offers a pool and seven restaurants, including the world's largest buffet. The renovated lobby is classy, but you cannot expect Strip accommodations at this price without compromise: the decor is typical chain-hotel style, with blue carpeting and blonde-wood furniture. Choose from 3,770 rooms and suites in the main hotel (the newest are in the West Tower) and motor lodge, or camp in the 399-site RV park, the Strip's only campground.

The Mirage

3400 Las Vegas Boulevard South; tel: 702-791-7111 or 800-627-6667; www.mirage.com; $–$$$$

The first of the Strip's post-50s themed resorts, the Polynesian Mirage is the best resort for nature lovers. Guests can enjoy waterfalls, a lagoon, and Siegfried & Roy's Secret Garden, home to white lions and tigers and a family of Atlantic bottlenose dolphins. Most of the 3,000 plus rooms and suites showcase marble and canopied beds; six have *lanais* (decks) with a private garden and pool; and eight are exclusive two- and three-bedroom villas. Spread across the resort are two pools, a spa, six fine-dining restaurants, eight casual-dining restaurants, and various bars and lounges.

Riviera Hotel and Casino

2901 Las Vegas Boulevard South, tel: 702-734-5110 or 800-634-6753; www.rivierahotel.com; $–$$

Built in 1955, the nine-story Riviera was the first high-rise hotel on the Strip and had Liberace as its original headlining act. Today, this affordable resort (reputedly haunted) has arguably seen better days but it's a real bargain. Its five towers contain 2,000 rooms, including 187 suites, petite suites, one- and two-bedroom penthouses, and a honeymoon suite. There are plenty of dining options, plus a pool, lighted tennis courts, spas, and in-house shows.

Sahara Hotel and Casino

2535 Las Vegas Boulevard South, tel: 702-737-2111 or 888-696-2121; www.saharavegas.com; $–$$$$

Still bearing its famous Moroccan motif, the revamped 1952-built Sahara now attracts motor-racing fans rather than celebrities, with its Cyber Speedway, Speed-the Ride, and NASCAR Cafe. The 1,720 rooms and suites are

Price for a double room for one night with breakfast:	
$$$$	over 300 US dollars
$$$	200–300 US dollars
$$	100–200 US dollars
$	below 100 US dollars

comfortable and reasonably priced; all have kingsize beds, high-speed Internet, and plenty of other amenities. For a blast from the past, the Coasters, the Platters, and the Drifters sing their hits nightly in the Congo Room.

TI – Treasure Island
3300 Las Vegas Boulevard South; tel: 702-894-7111 or 800-944-7444; www.treasureisland.com; $$$

A recent renovation has ditched the child-oriented motif in favor of a more grown-up theme. Both affordable and comfortable, the rooms are set within a Y-shaped tower, with the least-expensive rooms on the lower floors and the more expensive ones higher up.

Venetian Resort, Hotel, and Casino
3355 Las Vegas Boulevard South, tel: 702-414-1000 or 877-283-6423; www.venetian.com; $$–$$$$+

A gorgeous rendition of La Bella Italia, the all-suite Venetian is a super-resort aimed at those with very deep pockets. Marble, frescoes, and velvet abound and authentic gondolas ply a series of canals connected to exclusive shops, while street performers entertain in the replica St. Mark's Square. There's also the Guggenheim Hermitage Museum, designed by Rem Koolhaas, and 17 acclaimed restaurants that showcase talented chefs such as Emeril Lagasse and Wolfgang Puck. The 4,000 suites in the two 36-story towers average 700 sq ft (65 sq m) – the largest in Las Vegas. Amenities include kingsize canopied beds, sunken living rooms, wet bars, two TVs, high-speed Internet, and personal fax/printer/copier. The adjoining Palazzo Resort, under the same management, is scheduled to open shortly, expanding the size of the resort to include 30 restaurants, eight pools, and 3,000 additional suites.

Wynn Las Vegas
3131 Las Vegas Boulevard South, tel: 702-770-7000 or 888-320-9966; www.wynnlasvegas.com; $$$$+

Entrepreneur Steve Wynn's eponymous venture is the city's only Mobil and AAA Five-Star resort and reflects the owner's personal touch throughout, from the Wynn signature writ large on the outside to his personal introductions on the hotel's lavish website. The 2,700 suites all have floor-to-ceiling windows overlooking the onsite golf course and mountain lake, king-size beds with plush European linens and bedding, flat-screen TVs in both the living and bathroom areas, and high-speed Internet access. Stores here are upscale (think Prada and Chanel), and the nearly 20 restaurants are overseen by hot chefs such as Paul Bartolotta and Alessandro Stratta: the resort also has Las Vegas's most elegant buffet.

Southern Strip

Bally's Las Vegas
3645 Las Vegas Boulevard South; tel: 702-739-4111 or 800-634-3434; www.ballyslv.com; monorail: Bally's/Paris Las Vegas; $$$

Bally's is one of the oldest hotels on the Strip, but also one of the most over-

Above from far left: Art Nouveau elevator; expect all creature comfort at Vegas hotels.

Desert Mirage Inside the Mirage hotel is a stunning 20,000-gallon aquarium with an artificial coral reef populated by 90 species of marine life, including sharks, pufferfish, and angelfish.

Free Show
Ask for a room overlooking Bellagio's fountains as the musical accompanyment is simultaneously broadcast via the hotel's TV channel.

looked. Large rooms with a modern flair feature overstuffed furniture and subdued earth tones. The hotel has a beautiful pool area, which is perfect for hot days.

Bellagio

3600 Las Vegas Boulevard South; tel: 702-693-7111 or 888-987-6667; www.bellagioresort.com; $$$$

Occupying the site of the Dunes hotel and stealing the scene in the movie *Ocean's Eleven*, the Bellagio is one of the city's most lavish resorts. The beautiful accommodations are split between the main Italianate building and the newer Spa Tower, and even the standard rooms are satisfyingly plush and feature deluxe beds, huge marble bathrooms with tubs and showers big enough for two, and flatscreen TVs. There is an incredible array of fine dining options, including Prime, led by super-chef Jean-Georges Vongerichten, and the Picasso, designed by the artist's son Claude and with paintings on the walls estimated to be worth around $50 million. And on top of all, that there's a luxurious spa and a renowned golf course.

Caesars Palace

3570 Las Vegas Boulevard South; tel: 702-731-7110 or 800-634-6661; www. caesarspalace.com; $$–$$$$

This extravagant Las Vegas casino-hotel, a homage to Rome at its most decadent, has been pulling out all the stops since it opened in 1966. There are 2,400 elegant guest rooms and suites with fabulous bathrooms and plenty of amenities including butler service (at penthouse level), four pools set in extensive gardens, a floating cocktail lounge, 23 restaurants, including those run by celebrity chefs Bradley Ogden and Wolfgang Puck, a world-class spa, three casinos, a night club and show venue, and an exclusive high-end shopping arcade.

Excalibur

3850 Las Vegas Boulevard South; tel: 702-597-7777 or 877-750-5464; $$

Excalibur offers a fun Renaissance experience aimed at families and budget travelers. Considering the hotel's gaudy exterior, rooms are restrained, with wrought-iron accents over dark wood and contemporary touches of red, blue, and green. Restaurants include the huge (it seats 1,400 at a time) Roundtable Buffet, one of the best-value all-you-can-eat spots on the Strip.

Flamingo Las Vegas

3555 Las Vegas Boulevard South; tel: 702-733-3111 or 800-732-2111; www.flamingolv.com; monorail: Flamingo/Caesars Palace; $$–$$$

Mobster Bugsy Siegel would hardly recognize the hotel he built in 1946, giving the Las Vegas Strip its start.

Price for a double room for one night with breakfast:

$$$$	over 300 US dollars
$$$	200–300 US dollars
$$	100–200 US dollars
$	below 100 US dollars

Little has been left intact to hint at the Flamingo's shady past today, the newly refurbished rooms feature king-size beds and soft earth-tone decor. A full-wall mirror makes each room seem twice as big as it really is.

Four Seasons Hotel

3960 Las Vegas Boulevard South;
tel: 702-632-5000 or 877-632-5000;
www.fourseasons.com; $$$$

Exclusive, yet child-friendly, the Four Seasons is located on the Strip but feels a million miles away. The non-gaming hotel's 424 rooms, including 86 suites, are located in a five-story tower adjoining the Mandalay Bay, and it shares amenities with that resort. The guest accommodations have all you need to feel pampered, but there is also a vast pool, two Jacuzzis, and a full spa with 16 treatment rooms should you need more. Dining options range from casual to formal, and – most civilized – afternoon tea is served Monday to Thursday.

Harrah's

3475 Las Vegas Boulevard South;
tel: 702-369-5000 or 800-harrahs;
www.harrahs.com; monorail:
Harrah's/Imperial Palace; $$

Bright colors, light wood, and brass fixtures lend an upbeat feel to the accommodations in this venerable resort, which itself has a light, outdoorsy atmosphere. Jacuzzi tubs are available.

Luxor

3900 Las Vegas Boulevard South;
tel: 702-262-4000 or 800-288-1000;
www.luxor.com; $$

The rooms in the pyramid have one sloping glass wall overlooking the

Above from far left: whatever your taste, from classic to minimalist, you should be able to find a hotel to suit.

Left: by the pool at Caesars Palace.

main floor, and most have a shower but no tub (rooms in the towers do have tubs). There are family-friendly attractions and discount rates are often available. At time of printing, the hotel was due to be redesigned, and the former Egyptian theme abandoned.

Mandalay Bay Resort and Casino

3950 Las Vegas Boulevard South; tel: 702-632-7777 or 877-632-7000; www. mandalaybay.com; $$–$$$$
Strikingly elegant, this award-winning South Strip resort has many unusual features. The 3,800 rooms and suites are spacious and contemporary and include 100 House of Blues themed rooms on the 34th floor (the House of Blues concert hall is downstairs), as well as contemporary boutique-style suites in THEhotel. An 11-acre (4-ha) beach and lagoon area with a lazy river ride, three pools (only open to guests), Shark Reef, and wedding chapel are dotted around the lush grounds. Dining is exceptionally diverse, even by Las Vegas standards: celebrity chef Charlie Palmer works his culinary magic at Aureole, while Wolfgang Puck's does Italian at his Trattoria del Lupo – the first Italian restaurant opened by the now-ubiquitous super-

Price for a double room for one night with breakfast:	
$$$$	over 300 US dollars
$$$	200–300 US dollars
$$	100–200 US dollars
$	below 100 US dollars

chef – is also located here. In addition, there's also the China Grill, the Red Square Russian restaurant, several bars and lounges, and a large casino.

MGM Grand

3799 Las Vegas Boulevard South; tel: 702-891-7777 or 877-880-0880; www.mgmgrand.com; monorail: MGM Grand; $$$
Four distinct towers result in four different types of room themes. The nicest are in the Hollywood tower, with gold-speckled walls surrounding maple and cherry furniture. Gilded accents and framed photos of film stars add up to a classy experience. Restaurant choices are excellent here, too: expect beautiful presentation and top-quality ingredients at Craftsteak, where dishes are served under the watchful eye of chef Tom Colicchio, while at Stage Deli, a replica of a cool Manhattan delicatessen, you will be tempted by pastrami, salads, cheeses, and other deli delights. Other revered chefs with restaurants here include the French master Joël Robuchon, and Wolfgang Puck, whose Bar & Grill does high-class pizza and all-American cooking with a Californian twist.

Monte Carlo

3770 Las Vegas Boulevard South; tel: 702-730-7777 or 888-529-4828; www.montecarlo.com; $$–$$$
Striking in its understated European theme, this resort captures an air of continental beauty. The outdoor area is particularly lush, with a wave pool, waterfalls, and a river. Rooms are clas-

sically European in flavor and very comfortable. Television sets are concealed in armoires. Restaurants include André's, an elegant spot run by award-winning chef André Rochat.

New York New York

3790 Las Vegas Boulevard South; tel: 702-740-6969 or 866-815-4365; www.nynyhotelcasino.com; $$$

Taking theming to its extreme, rooms here are done in 62 styles, all related to the "Big Apple." Art Deco is the overall inspiration, with round-top furnishings and inlaid wood galore. On average, the rooms are small, but the overall experience is pleasant. Eating options include the America restaurant, which (not surprisingly) serves up home-grown dishes from buffalo wings to Santa Fe smothered chicken, and the ESPN Zone, an entertainment complex within which you can get such all-American favorites as ribs and steak sandwiches.

Paris Las Vegas

3655 Las Vegas Boulevard South; tel: 702-946-7000 or 888-266-5687; www.parislasvegas.com; $–$$$$

This reimagined Paris in the Mojave Desert, complete with detailed replicas of the Arc de Triomphe, the façades of the Louvre, the Paris Opera House, L'Hotel de Ville, and a 50-story, half-scale Eiffel Tower, looks and feels, dare we say it, surprisingly authentic. The landmark Eiffel Tower (open for tours and great views of Las Vegas) is the hotel's focal point, with nine restaurants serving classic French

cuisine (including Mon Ami Gabi and the Eiffel Tower Restaurant), shops, and a casino all in its shadow. The 3,200 rooms and suites are spacious and feature marble and custom-made vaguely French, Regency-style furniture. There's a pool, a large, inviting Balinese-style spa, a fitness center, and a wedding chapel that you might want to use if you have a great night out at the on-site nightclub and are feeling particularly romantic.

Tropicana Resort and Casino

3801 Las Vegas Boulevard South; tel: 702-739-2222 or 800-634-4000; fwww.tropicanalv.com; monorail: MGM Grand; $–$$$

Aimed at adult travelers, the Tropicana is one of the few hotels dating back to the "old" Las Vegas of the 1950s and its rates are among the lowest on the Strip. The motif is somewhat Polynesian. The standard rooms are light, plain and functional, accented by bedspreads and draperies in bright tropical designs. Many on the lower floors look out onto lush foliage that surrounds the pool and offers a buffer against the urban clamor. The tropical pool area has swim-up blackjack tables.

Beyond the Strip

Artisan Hotel

1501 West Sahara Avenue; tel: 702-214-4000 or 800-554-4092; www.theartisanhotel.com; $$–$$$$

The small Art Deco-style Artisan is located away from the Strip and is the closest Las Vegas gets to a boutique hotel. It is perfect for non-gamblers and

business travelers seeking restful sur-
roundings, taking its inspiration from
European hotels, and incorporating
soothing low lighting throughout as
well as original art by Van Gogh, Marc
Chagall, and other celebrated artists.
The 64 rooms are all spacious, non-
smoking, and include wireless Internet.
There is a pool, complimentary daily
wine reception at 4:30pm in the lobby,
a bar, casual cafe, and an attractive fine-
dining restaurant.

Blue Moon Resort

2651 Westwood Drive; tel: 702-361-
9099 or 866-796-9194; www.
bluemoonlasvegas.com; $$$
The only gay men's resort in Las Vegas
is a cluster of elegantly transformed
buildings just off the Sahara Avenue
exit from Interstate 15, approximately
2 miles (3km) from the Strip. It might
resemble a budget motel from the out-
side, but inside the three-story, 45-unit
complex you'll find super-sleek guest
rooms and suites with refrigerators,
big-screen TVs, CD sound systems
with iPod ports, romantic overhead
spot lighting, floor-to-ceiling curtains,
and large beds with pillow-top mat-
tresses. Closed-circuit Blue Moon
Radio pipes in chill and dance music
or Sirius Satellite's Out Q Channel,
and wireless Internet access lets you
use the password you receive at check-
in to chat live on your laptop with
other guests. Besides the pool, facili-
ties include a steam room and a
10-man jacuzzi grotto, and massage
services are available. The resort hosts
Sunday afternoon poolside barbecues

as well as lots of special events to suit
most tastes – check their website for
dates.

Golden Gate Hotel

1 Fremont Street; tel: 702-385-1906
or 800-426-1906; www.golden
gatecasino.com; $
This 1906-built, 106-room hotel and
casino in Downtown is the oldest and
smallest hotel in Vegas – now dwarfed
by the Golden Nugget Casino and the
Fremont Street Experience. Rooms are
standard, with just a few mod-cons.

Greek Isles Hotel and Casino

305 Convention Center Drive; tel:
702-952-8000 or 800-633-1777;
www.greekislesvegas.com; $$
This business-oriented hotel is char-
acterized by its Greek decor, with a
fountain in the lobby and an indoor
"sidewalk" taverna. There's an onsite
showroom and comedy lounge, wedding chapel, plus exercise facilities,
business services, 24-hour pool, and
restaurant. Rooms are spacious, with
blackout drapes. Suites and "mini-
suites" have views of the mountains or
the Strip, which is an easy walk away.

Hard Rock Hotel and Casino

4455 Paradise Road; tel: 702-693-
5000 or 800-473-7625; www.
hardrockhotel.com; $–$$$$
Situated behind a branch of the world-
famous Hard Rock Cafe, with its
original rock 'n' roll memorabilia,
high-priced hamburgers, and wait-
resses dressed in 1950s-style uniforms,
the Hard Rock Hotel and Casino

attracts a celebrity clientele. There are poolside concerts starring today's best musicians, intimate shows in the small concert hall and lounge, a popular see-and-be-seen pool area, a spa and health club, and five restaurants serving everything from comfort food and tacos to Las Vegas's best Japanese food in fashionable Nobu. The 600 ultra-modern rooms and suites have wide-screen plasma TVs and Bose CD systems. Otherwise, the furnishings are so minimal that even the rowdiest of rock bands would have a hard time trashing them.

Hooters Casino Hotel

115 East Tropicana Avenue; tel:
702-739-9000 or 866-584-6687;
www.hooterscasinohotel.com; $–$$
Based on the sports bar/restaurants featuring well-endowed Hooters Girls clad in skimpy T-shirts and bikinis, this party-loving hotel offers plenty of fun-in-the-sun activities for the lads. The 650 rooms and suites located in the hotel, tower, or bungalows have a relaxed tropical Florida theme.

Motel 6

195 East Tropicana Avenue;
tel: 702-798-0728; $–$$
Location is everything at this low-rise motel next to Hooters and the Tropicana, within a few blocks' walk of the coolest casino resorts on the Las Vegas Strip. The rooms are as spartan as you'd expect at a Motel 6, and the desk clerk sits behind steel bars. But, if all you really need is an air-conditioned, no-frills place to change clothes, with

a bed, a shower, a phone and a TV set, this is it. (Note that the motel does have a swimming pool.) Room rates vary dramatically from day to day. During the week, you may pay about the same as a semi-private room at a youth hostel, but on weekends, expect to pay much more.

Ritz-Carlton–Lake Las Vegas

1610 Lake Las Vegas Parkway,
Henderson; tel: 702-567-4700;
www.ritzcarlton.com; $$$$
To nourish your romance, find a private place where you can be together far from the tourist hordes. Lake Las Vegas feels about as far removed from everyday reality as a resort can. On the road from Henderson to Lake Mead, 20 to 30 minutes' drive from the Strip, this large artificial lake is surrounded by palm trees, verdant lawns, a golf course, three luxury hotels, and hundreds of private low-rise condos, townhouses, and villas. The Ritz-Carlton, the classiest hotel on the lake, offers spa packages that include one night's stay, breakfast, and two massages from under $450. (If that's not enough to impress, the hotel also offers a weekend complete with yacht, helicopter, champagne bath, roses, diamonds, and a singing gondolier – all for $100,000. Whether anyone has ever taken them up on this deal is a closely guarded secret.) This is a small hotel by Las Vegas standards, with just 349 guest rooms and suites of various sizes, all luxuriously appointed in soft desert color schemes. Ask for a room with a lake view, if your budget allows.

Above from far left: a fruity theme; Wynn Las Vegas.

Lake Las Vegas
There are no fewer than nine locations where you can get married in the Lake Las Vegas resort, including a floating stage that can be anchored in any chosen lake locale.

Northern Strip

AquaKnox

The Venetian, 3355 Las Vegas Boulevard South; tel: 702-414-2220; www.venetian.com; Sun–Thur 5:30–11pm, Fri–Sat 5:30–11.30pm; $$$$
Celebrity chef Tom Moloney, formerly with the Wolfgang Puck restaurant empire, flies in fresh seafood daily from around the world to prepare dishes such as tuna tataki and wild Tasmanian sea trout. It's all served up in a cool, ocean-hued setting.

Delmonico's Steakhouse

Venetian, Casino Level, 3355 Las Vegas Boulevard South; tel: 702-414-3737; www.venetian.com; daily 11:30am–1:45pm and 5–10pm; $$$$
Emeril Lagasse's Delmonico's Steakhouse delivers on hearty, imaginative, creole-infused meat-and-potatoes fare and even richer desserts known and loved by millions because of the celebrity chef's popular TV shows. Among the signature dishes are starters including steak tartare and gumbo, entrees such as pork chops with bacon-wrapped shrimp and bourbon smashed sweet potatoes, and charbroiled dry-aged beef sirloin accompanied by bacon-cheddar twice-baked potato, Creole tomato glaze, and

Price guide for an average two-course meal for one with a glass of house wine:

$$$$	over $60
$$$	$40–60
$$	$20–40
$	under $20

horseradish cream. Desserts such as banana bread pudding with ice cream and fudge sauce and whisky creme brulee are no less impressive. Reservations are necessary. Lagasse also has a creole fish house, Emeril's, in the MGM Grand.

Onda

The Mirage, 3400 Las Vegas Boulevard South; tel: 702-791-7223; www.mirage.com; daily 5–10:30pm; $$$
This "*ristorante* and wine lounge" has consistently been voted Las Vegas's Best Italian Restaurant in newspaper surveys. The menu mixes regional and classic Italian dishes with North American innovations, featuring selections such as capellini with scallops, veal marsala, and softshell crabs.

Southern Strip

Aureole

Mandalay Bay, 3950 Las Vegas Boulevard South; tel: 702-632-7401; www.aureolelv.com; daily 6–10pm; $$$$
Dinner theater takes on new meaning in Las Vegas's best restaurants, where gourmet food meets out-of-this-world fantasy settings, and it's hard to beat the drama of chef Charlie Palmer's Aureole. Its centerpiece is a glassed-in, 42-ft (13-m) wine tower containing 10,000 bottles of wine, where "the show" consists of watching "wine angels" ascend and find your bottle of wine (ordered via electric sommelier, no less), then descend with your chosen vintage. The food here scales other heights. A lavish, prix-fixe, seven-course meal might

include a duet of ahi tuna, three-cheese ravioli accompanied by Dungeness crab, roasted Chilean sea bass, Sonoma squab and seared foie gras, filet mignon and shepherd's pie, and tarte Tatin. Thankfully, an à-la-carte menu is available for those with both budgets and appetites closer to the ground. Either way, save room for one of the out-of-this-world desserts. Reservations highly recommended. Formal dress.

Border Grill

Beach Level, Mandalay Bay Hotel; 3950 Las Vegas Boulevard South; tel: 702-632-7403; www.bordergrill.com; daily 11:30am–10pm (until 11pm Fri–Sat); $$

With its perfect poolside setting, bright colors, and hip, fun food, Border Grill offers a cuisine inspired by the spices and flavors of Mexico and beyond. US TV chefs Mary Sue Milliken and Susan Feniger personally oversee this branch of their flagship Santa Monica restaurant, so bet on quality and consistency. Try chicken tortilla soup, a selection of *tamales*, *cochinita pibil*, a Yucatecan pork dish slow-cooked in banana leaves, and *pescado Veracruzana*, halibut in a garlic and wine broth with tomatoes and olives. The *taquería* upstairs offers takeout tacos filled with *carne asada*, beans, cheese, fish, and beef brisket. Standout dining at great prices in an airy atmosphere.

Bradley Ogden

Caesar's Palace, 3570 Las Vegas Boulevard South; tel: 702-731-7410; www.larkcreek.com; daily 5–11pm; $$$$

Drawing inspiration from fresh, locally grown foods flown in from boutique farmers from Northern California and beyond, San Francisco top chef-restaurateur Bradley Ogden and his son personally oversee his Las Vegas kitchen. Here they conjure up elegant, New American dishes such as hot and cold foie gras with kumquats, seared scallop in spring onions soup, and prime rib with Yukon potato pavé and Merlot sauce. A well-chosen wine list and gorgeous dining room make this a great place for a special meal.

Above from far left: too good to eat; something for the kids; a healthier option; unmissable Mexican food.

Additional Restaurants
For further selected restaurants, see the food and drink boxes within the tours (pp.28–95).

Left: Aureole, at the Mandalay Bay.

Celebrity Chefs
The arrival of
celebrity chefs has
transformed Las
Vegas dining, as
more and more
accolades and
diamond stars are
awarded to local
restaurants. Indeed,
Tim Zagat, of the
Zagat restaurant
guides, predicts
that in future,
celebrity chefs will
be just as likely to
make their names
in Las Vegas as in
New York or
Los Angeles.

Charlie Palmer Steakhouse

Four Seasons Hotel, 3960 Las
Vegas Boulevard South; tel: 702-
362-5000; www.charliepalmer.com;
daily 5:30–10:30pm; $$$$

Celebrity chef Charlie Palmer presents
most of his signature dishes here, such
as wood-grilled filet mignon and an
astonishing 48-oz New York strip steak
for die-hard carnivores. Seafood or
family-style side dishes are available to
non-meat eaters. Premises are spacious,
with a clubby atmosphere accented by
rich polished wood.

Craftsteak

MGM Grand, 3799 Las Vegas Boulevard South; tel: 702-891-7318;
www.craftrestaurant.com; Sun–Mon
5.30–10pm, Tue–Thur 5–10pm,
Fri–Sat 5–10.30pm; $$$$

Using simple ingredients flown in
fresh daily from small family farms,
award-winning chef Tom Colicchio
creates striking presentations of fla-
vorful dishes including lobster, wild
king salmon, and the house specialty,
grilled Kobe skirt steak. There is also
an extensive wine list.

Eiffel Tower Restaurant

Paris Las Vegas, 3655 Las Vegas
Boulevard South; www.eiffeltower
restaurant.com; tel: 702-948-6937;
daily 5:30–10pm; $$$$

Chef J. Joho's gourmet Gallic entrées
are served in an elegant, contemporary
atmosphere. Expect dishes such as blue
cheese soufflé pudding, tournedos
Rossini with foie gras and truffle sauce,
and a spectacular seafood platter.

Fix

Bellagio, 3600 Las Vegas Boulevard
South; tel: 702-693-8400; www.
bellagio.com; Sun–Thur 5pm–midnight, Fri–Sat 5pm–2am; $$$$

This huge, architecturally impressive
space is a combined bar, club and
restaurant serving elegant American
comfort food. The menu includes
tomato soup, mushroom bisque, crab
cakes, sashimi, caviar, roast chicken,
Kobe beef, ribeye steak, milk shakes,
and root-beer floats. A good place for
a martini or mojito and a bite to eat
while watching the casino action.

Fusia

The Luxor, 3900 Las Vegas Boulevard South; tel: 702-262-4000;
www.luxor.com; daily 6–11pm; $$

Even the most jaded of pan-Asian epi-
cures are sure to find something new
and unique on the menu of chef
Gerald Trujillo's new restaurant, where
presentations emphasize spice, color,
and aroma. Try the spiced Indonesian
crab stack or the Nigiri-style sushi.

L'Atelier de Joel Robuchon

MGM Grand, 3799 Las Vegas Boule-
vard South; tel: 702-891-7349;
www.mgmgrand.com; Mon–Thur 5–
10:30pm, Sat–Sun 5–11:30pm; $$$$

Very expensive even for a Las Vegas
signature restaurant, L'Atelier serves
either à la carte, with entrees such as
suckling pig confit and sea bass on a
bed of baby leeks, or from *dégustation*
and *découverte* menus that offer arrays
of tasting portions. The setting is
dramatically hip.

Les Artistes Steakhouse

Paris Las Vegas, 3655 Las Vegas Boulevard South; tel: 702-946-3908; www.parislasvegas.com; daily 5:30–10:30pm; $$

French-inspired versions of steak and seafood fare, such as a bone-in filet mignon with Bearnaise sauce accompanied by a stuffed Provençale tomato, are served in one of the city's most fascinating restaurant settings, its walls covered by dozens of French Impressionist paintings.

Nobhill

MGM Grand, 3799 Las Vegas Boulevard South; tel: 702-891-7220; www.mgmgrand.com; Sun–Thur 5:30–10pm, Fri–Sat 5:30–10:30pm; $$$$

Award-winning San Francisco chef Michael Mina evokes the culinary traditions of the City by the Bay in this warm, intimate restaurant. Main courses include North Beach cioppino and Japanese snapper with butternut squash risotto and chanterelle mushrooms. There is a unique lobster tasting menu featuring four different lobster dishes, as well as fruit, cheese, and wine pairings.

Prime Steakhouse

Bellagio, 3600 Las Vegas Boulevard South; tel: 702-693-7111; www.bellagio.com; daily 5–10pm; $$$

Dark wood panelling and dining booths secluded by ornate tapestry curtains create a romantic setting in which to savor master chef Jean-Georges Vongerichten's works of culinary art. Though it styles itself as a steakhouse, the restaurant's menu features only a couple of beef dishes among more creative offerings such as seared tuna *au poivre* with wasabi-mashed potato and steamed bok choy.

Spago

Forum Shops at Caesars Palace; 3500 Las Vegas Boulevard South; tel: 702-369-6300; www.wolfgang puck.com; Sun–Thur 11am–11pm, Fri–Sat 11am–midnight; $$–$$$

Visionary pizza meister Wolfgang Puck began Las Vegas's gourmet dining in 1992, and he's still at the forefront of fine dining in the city with no fewer than four restaurants, two of which – Spago and Chinois – are found in Caesars Palace. Spago is a multistory, art-filled, fine-dining restaurant fronted by a casual, less-expensive eatery with sidewalk dining (also at lunchtime) and good casino watching. Smoked salmon pizza remains Puck's signature dish, as well as comfort foods such as pancetta-bacon-wrapped meatloaf and mashed potatoes. In season yellow-fin tuna, crab cakes, short ribs, and snapper head up the dinner choices. Puck attempts to use organic meats, eggs, dairy, and produce whenever available. Desserts are rich and decadent. Reservations are strongly recommended.

Buffets

The buffet tradition began in the 1940s at the El Rancho Vegas Hotel, when the owner, Beldon Katleman, introduced an "all you can eat for a dollar" Midnight Chuck Wagon Buffet to keep customers in his casino after the second floor show ended. The idea was copied by other casinos, then extended to include breakfast, lunch, and dinner.

Price guide for an average two-course meal for one with a glass of house wine:	
$$$$	over $60
$$$	$40–60
$$	$20–40
$	under $20

Andre's

401 South 6th Street; tel: 702-385-5016; www.andrelv.com; Mon–Sat 6–11pm; $$$

If you definitively do not want to eat a stratospherically expensive meal inside a casino resort surrounded by people in shorts and flip flops, this chic French restaurant is for you. Situated in a 1930s Provençal-style home, André's was the city's first successful French restaurant and offers an intimate dining experience – like eating a fine meal in an elegant home lovingly cooked by a friend who happens to be a gourmet chef. Try the snails, scallops, mustard-crusted rack of lamb, and braised veal cheek. The sweet dessert soufflés are out of this world, and the wine cellar is extensive. Reservations are essential. Formal attire is suggested.

Golden Steer Steakhouse

308 West Sahara Avenue; tel: 702-384-4470; www.goldensteerlv.com; daily 5–11pm; $$$

For nearly half a century, the Golden Steer has been serving seafood and tasty steaks to locals and visitors in the know, including Vegas legends Frank Sinatra and his Rat Pack, Elvis Presley, and John Wayne. There are historic photo-

graphs on the walls, and the waiters wear snappy tuxedos.

Little Buddha

Palms, 4321 West Flamingo Road; tel: 702-942-7778; www.littlebuddha lasvegas.com; Sun–Thur 5.30–11pm, Fri–Sat 5.30pm–midnight; $$

Inexpensive and inexorably hip, this offshoot of the famous Buddha Bar in Paris serves terrific sushi and other Asian Fusion faves to a hypnotic, chill-out, world-music beat.

Lotus of Siam

953 East Sahara Avenue; tel: 702-753-3033; www.saipinchutima.com; Mon–Fri 11.30am–2.30pm, Mon–Thur 5.30– 9.30pm, Fri–Sun 5.30–10pm; $$

Justin Gold of *Gourmet* magazine has called this the "single best Thai restaurant in North America." The lengthy menu includes not only well-known dishes such as coconut curries, but also the little-known cuisine of north-eastern Thailand such as *kang-ka-noon*, spicy young jackfruit curry with a choice of pork, chicken, or smoked fish flakes.

Mayflower Cuisinier

4750 West Sahara Avenue; tel: 702-870-8432; Mon–Fri 11am–3pm, Mon–Thur 5–10pm, Fri–Sat 5–11pm, closed Sun; $$

Contemporary California-style Chinese cuisine with French influences sets this one apart. Typical of the mixed-culture cuisine is the kung pao seafood medley of shrimp, scallops, and salmon. Patio dining is available.

Play to Eat
Alongside paying customers at hotel restaurants are a new breed of diners. Gamblers are regularly rewarded for their play by pit bosses scribbling out "comps" (complimentary tickets) for the hotel's on-site restaurants. The level of comp depends upon the level of play, so everyone – low-rollers to big spenders – can be accommodated.

Price guide for an average two-course meal for one with a glass of house wine:	
$$$$	over $60
$$$	$40–60
$$	$20–40
$	under $20

Pamplemousse

400 East Sahara Avenue, tel. 702 733-2066; www.pamplemousse restaurant.com; daily 5:30–10:30pm; $$$$

One of Las Vegas's most romantic restaurants for more than 30 years, Pamplemousse combines the ambience of a French country inn with largely French cuisine-inspired dishes, such as onion soup, mussels, and veal medallions with mustard sauce. You can select from the regular menu (not printed, only recited tableside by the waiter), an "epicurean" five-course prix-fixe dinner, or a "gourmet" menu shared by a minimum of 10 guests.

Rosemary's

8125 West Sahara Avenue, Suite 110; tel: 702-869-2251; www.rosemarys restaurant.com; Mon–Fri 11.30am– 2.30pm and 5.30–10.30pm, Sat–Sun 5.30–10.30pm; $$

Michael Jordan (formerly of New Orleans eateries including Emeril's) and his wife Wendy have created an attractive, art-filled, off-Strip restaurant that, despite its mall location, consistently tops local Favorite Gourmet and Romantic Restaurant polls. A 30-seat full-service bar and eight-seat counter overlooking the kitchen are a popular local gathering spot for tapas and drinks. But what brings people back again and again is the inspired, seasonal, three-course, prix-fixe dinner menu, derived from regionally grown foods that reflect Jordan's unique take on steak and seafood, salads, and desserts. Reservations recommended.

Roy's Las Vegas

8701 West Charleston Boulevard (Fort Apache Road),Summorlin; tel: 702-838-3620; www.roysrestaurant. com; daily 5:30–10pm; $$$

Another superb reincarnation of a famed restaurant – this time, Roy's Honolulu, the elegant Asian Fusion seafood eatery on the Hawaiian island of Oahu. Among the signature dishes are blackened ahi tuna, hibachi-grilled salmon in ponzu sauce, and Szechuan-spiced baby back pork ribs. Roy's has another location offstrip at 620 East Flamingo Road; tel: 702-691-2053.

The VooDoo Steak and Lounge

Rio, 3700 West Flamingo Road; tel: 702-247-7800; www.riolasvegas. com; daily 5–11pm; $$

Fifty floors up, with a view overlooking all of Las Vegas, this restaurant serves up spicy Creole and Cajun specialties, including daily specials and a *ménage à trois* of filet mignon, lobster, and prawns, with Bananas Foster for dessert. You might like to start or finish your meal with cocktails in the lounge.

Above from far left: for the all-American finishing touch; neon cocktail; Top of the World Restaurant, in the Stratosphere Tower *(see p.52);* meaty feast.

Left: a huge number of top celebrity chefs have Las Vegas restaurants, where you can so expect beautifully prepared and presented dishes.

CREDITS

Insight Step by Step Las Vegas
Written by: Richard Harris
Series Editor: Clare Peel
Cartography Editor: James Macdonald
Picture Managers: Hilary Genin,
Steve Lawrence
Art Editor: Ian Spick
Production: Kenneth Chan
Editorial Director: Brian Bell

Photography by: Apa: Abe Nowitz, Richard Nowitz, Britta Jaschinski except: AKG 23TL; Alamy 16T, 26–7, 91T, 92T, 92B, 109B; Corbis 8/9, 11, 23TR, 75B, 95TR; Courtesy of Caesars Palace 85B; Getty 17B, 22TL, 31TL, 41B, 61TL, 61TR, 68TL, 89, 96–7; Ronald Grant Archive 22TR; Dave Hanson 32TR; Catherine Karnow 90B; Keystone USA/Rex Features 95B; Vincent Kostiw/AlsaceTalent.com 38TL, 38TR, 38 margin top, center, bottom, 39TR; Las Vegas News Bureau/LVCVA 25, 28CL, 41TL; Courtesy of Frank Marino 64; Courtesy of Marjorie Barrick Museum of Natural History 34TR; Mary Evans Picture Library 24T; Courtesy of MGM Mirage 33TR, 34TL, 34 margin top, center, bottom, 35TR, 71TL, 44 margin top, 44 margin bottom, 47T, 78TR, 88TR, 89TL, 119B, 121TL; Gail Mooney 32TL; Courtesy of Paymon's Mediterranean Café/Hookah Lounge 64TL; Tamasz Rossa/Costumes by Thierry Mugler/© Cirque du Soleil Inc; Toney Smith 33TL; Mike Stotts/WpN 35TL; Topham Picturepoint 24CL; UPPA/Photoshot 55B; Michael Walker 75T.

Cover: main image: Timothy Hursley/Superstock; front left: Britta Jaschinski; front right: Abe Nowitz.

Printed by: Insight Print Services (Pte) Ltd, 38 Joo Koon Road, Singapore 628990

© 2008 Apa Publications GmbH & Co. Verlag KG (Singapore branch)

CONTACTING THE EDITORS

We would appreciate it if readers would alert us to errors or outdated information by writing to us at insight@apaguide.co.uk or Apa Publications, PO Box 7910, London SE1 1WE, UK.

www.insightguides.com

DISTRIBUTION

Worldwide
**Apa Publications GmbH & Co. Verlag KG
(Singapore branch)**
38 Joo Koon Road
Singapore 628990
Tel: (65) 6865 1600
Fax: (65) 6861 6438

UK and Ireland
GeoCenter International Ltd
Meridian House, Churchill Way West
Basingstoke, Hampshire, RG21 6YR
Tel: (44) 1256 817 987
Fax: (44) 1256 817 988

United States
Langenscheidt Publishers, Inc.
36–36 33rd Street, 4th Floor
Long Island City, NY 11106
Tel: (1) 718 784 0055
Fax: (1) 718 784 0640

Australia
Universal Publishers
1 Waterloo Road
Macquarie Park
NSW 2113
Tel: (61) 2 9857 3700
Fax: (61) 2 9888 9074

New Zealand
Hema Maps New Zealand Ltd (HNZ)
Unit D, 24 Ra ORA Drive
East Tamaki, Auckland
Tel: (64) 9 273 6459
Fax: (64) 9 273 6479

INDEX

A

accommodations 110–17
Adventuredome 48
age restrictions 98
Airmail 22
airports 106
All-Natural Las Vegas 32–5
alcohol 15
Amazing Colossal Man, The 22
aquarium 33
Arboretum 34
Arizona 94
ArtAbout 38
Artisan Hotel 56–8, 115
Artistic Las Vegas 36–41
Arts District, 18b 12, 36–9
Arts Factory 38
Atlatl Rock 91
automobile collection 44

B

Bally's 23, 43, 111
Bellagio 12, 36, 40, 45, 88,
    112, 120, 121
Bernard K. Passman Gallery 37
Big Shot (ride) 53
Bill's 43
Binion's 4, 29
birdwatching 104
blackjack 18, 81–2
Blue Moon Resort 61, 63, 116
Boulder City 95
Boulevard, The 17
bowling 65
boxing 82
Budget Las Vegas 86–9
budgeting 98
buffets 15, 121
bus (Greyhound) 106

C

Caesars Palace 14, 42, 44, 62,
    78–85, 112, 119, 121

Forum Shops 45, 57, 62
    Garden of the Gods 85
Cage, Nicholas 23
car rental 106
Carluccio's Tivoli Gardens 64
Casino 22
celebrity chefs 14, 120
Chihuly, Dale 40, 41
children 48–51, 98–9
Chinatown 45
Chippendales 56–9
cigars 66
Circus Circus 12, 48–9,
    50, 87–8, 110
Cirque du Soleil 41, 55, 71
Classic Las Vegas 28–31
climate 12, 99
clothing 99
Comedy Stop at the Trop 67
Con Air 23
concerts 40
Contemporary Arts
    Collective 39
Cooler, The 23
cowboys 74–5, 77
craps 18, 80
crime and safety 99
CSI: Las Vegas 23
currency and taxes 99–100
customs 100

D

Diamonds Are Forever 22–3
Dietrich, Marlene 25
Dion, Celine 105
disabled travellers 100, 101
Downtown 12, 28–9, 72–3, 89
driving 15, 106
Dunes, The 45
Dust Gallery 39

E

electricity 100
embassies 100

emergencies 100
environment 12, 90, 100
Ethel's Chocolate Lounge 58
Ethel M's Chocolate Factory
    and Botanical Gardens 70
Evans, Keith 35
Excalibur 50–1, 70, 112

F

Farrow, Mia 21
Fashion Show Mall 16, 56–7, 61
Film Critics Society 23
Fiori di Como 40
First Friday 38
Flamingo Las Vegas
    30, 34, 43, 88, 112
Flamingo Wildlife Habitat 34
Floyd Lamb State Park 74–5
Flyaway Indoor Skydiving 52
Folies Bergere 11, 67
food and drink 14–15, 80, 103,
    118–23
Forum Shops 45, 57, 62
fountain show 45
Four Seasons 113, 120
Foxx, Red 28
Fremont, John C. 24
Fremont Street 12, 24–5,
    28–9, 86

G

Gable, Clark 22
Gabor, Zsa Zsa 21
Gamblers' Las Vegas 78–85
gambling 18–19, 78–85
gambling etiquette 101
gambling help 101
Garden of the Gods 84
Gardner, Ava 21
gay issues 60–4, 101
Gay Las Vegas 60–4
Get Carter 23
Godfather, The 22
Godt-Cleary Arts 39

Golden Gate Hotel **72–3, 116**
Golden Nugget **31**
golf **65**
gondola ride **51**
Grand Canal **36**
Grand Canal Shoppes **44, 57**
Grand Canyon West **93–5, 101**
   Skywalk **95**
Greek Isles Hotel **31, 102, 116**
Guggenheim-Hermitage
   Museum **37, 44**
guided tours **101–2**
Gun Store **66**

H

Hard Rock **116**
Harrah's **51, 113**
Haunted Nevada **28**
Havana Cigar Company **66–7**
Haymes, Dick **21**
Hayworth, Rita **21**
Hazards of Helen, The **22**
health **102–3**
helicopter tours **54**
Henderson **90**
hiking **91–2, 104**
history **24–5**
Hofbräuhaus **15, 42, 46**
Honey, I Blew Up the Kid **22**
Hooters **66, 117**
Hoover Dam **93–4**
   Visitors' Center **94**
horse riding **76–7**
hospitals **103**
hot-air balloons **102**
hotel listings **110–17**
hours and holidays **104**
Hualapai Indians **93, 95**
Hualapai Ranch **95**

I

Imperial Palace **43–4, 88**
impersonators **31, 64**
Insanity (ride) **53**
International Las Vegas **42–7**
internet cafes **108**

J

John, Elton **62, 105**

K

Kà **55**
keno **19**
Kerkorian, Kirk **30**

L

Ladies-Only Vegas **56–9**
Lady Luck **22**
Lake Las Vegas **12, 69**
Lake Mead **12, 90–2**
Lake Mead National
   Recreation Area **90–1**
Larry's Hideaway **77**
Las Vegas (NBC Series) **23**
Las Vegas Cyber Speedway **54**
Las Vegas Hilton **50**
Las Vegas National Golf Club **65**
Las Vegas Natural History
   Museum **76**
Las Vegas Philharmonic **40**
Las Vegas Premium Outlets **17**
Las Vegas Zoo **34**
Le Rêve **41, 58**
Leaving Las Vegas **23**
lesbian issues **60–4, 101**
Liberace **11, 26, 61, 63, 102**
   Liberace Museum **63**
limousines **70**
Little Church of the West **21**
Little White Chapel **21**
Lost City Museum **92**
Lost Vegas Gambling Museum
   and Shop **29**
Lucky Strike Lanes **66**
Lucky You **23**
Luxor **46, 89, 113, 120**
   King Tut Museum **46**

M

Macy, William H. **23**
Madame Tussaud's **50–1**

magicians **51**
Mandalay Bay **46–7, 70, 114,
   118, 119**
   Shark Reef **33–5**
Manhattan Express **55**
Marjorie Barrick Museum
   and Arboretum **34**
Marino, Frank **64**
Mars Attacks **22**
media **104**
MGM Grand **50, 55, 88,
   114, 120, 121**
   Lion Habitat **35, 50**
mini-baccarat **84**
Mirage **32–4, 42, 44, 88, 110, 118**
   Dolphin Habitat **33**
   Siegfried & Roy **33**
   tropical rainforest **33–4**
   white tigers **32**
Misfits, The **22**
Moapa Indian Reservation **92**
Mojave desert **12, 34**
monorail **13, 54–5**
Monroe, Marilyn **22**
Monte Carlo hotel **45, 114**
Montelago **69**
Mount Charleston **12**
Mouse's Tank **91**
movies **22–3**

N

NASCAR Cafe **54**
National Finals Rodeo **74**
Neonopolis **17, 29**
Nevada state boundary **94**
Nevada State Museum
   and Historical Society **74**
New York New York **34, 42, 46,
   55, 70–1, 88–9, 115**
Next **23**
Northern Club **25**

O

Ocean's Eleven **22–3**
Old Las Vegas Mormon
   State Park **73–4**

Old Mormon Fort **73, 74**
Old West Las Vegas
72–7
outdoor activities **104–5**
overview **8–25**

P

Pai Gow poker **83**
Paris Las Vegas **14, 16, 21, 42–3, 55, 57–8, 68, 88, 115, 120, 121**
passports **107–8**
people **13**
petroglyphs **91**
Picasso, Pablo **40–1**
Pink E's **65–6**
poker **19, 83–4**
pool **65**
post **105**
Presley, Elvis **11, 20, 22, 28, 51, 102**
Pride Week **62, 101**
public transportation **107**
Puck, Wolfgang **14**

R

Rat Pack **22–3, 26–7, 31, 44**
The Rat Pack is Back **31**
recommended tours **6–7**
Red Rock Canyon **76**
open-air theater **76**
Red Square **70**
Regis Galerie **36–7**
restaurants **118–23**
Rio All-Suite Las Vegas
Hotel and Casino **58–9, 66**
Ritz-Carlton **68–9, 117**
Rivers, Frank **61**
Riviera **29, 63–4, 110**
La Cage **64**
rodeo **74**
Rogers Warm Spring **91**
Romantic Las Vegas
68–71
Rooney, Mickey **21**
roulette **19, 81**

S

S2 Art Group **38–9**
Sahara **53–5, 86, 110**
Sanders, George **21**
Sands Hotel **44**
Scorsese, Martin **22**
shopping **16–17, 57, 88**
malls **16–17, 56–7, 61**
outlets **17, 57**
Siegel, Bugsy **22, 25, 28, 30, 102**
Siegfried & Roy **33, 61**
Sinatra, Frank **21, 22, 24, 31, 44**
skiing **105**
skydiving **52**
Skywalk (Grand Canyon) **95**
slot machines **79–80, 84**
Slots a Fun **12, 86–7**
smoking **66, 105**
Snake Eyes **23**
Spamalot **47**
spas **56, 58, 69**
Spears, Britney **21, 50**
Speed: The Ride **54**
sports books **19, 82**
Spring Mountain Ranch **76–7**
Star Trek – The Experience **50**
Stratosphere Tower **13, 52–4, 68, 70**
Streisand, Barbra **11**
Strip, the **10**
Superbowl **74**

T

telephones **105**
Thrill-Seekers' Las Vegas
52–5
tickets **105–6**
time differences **106**
tipping **106**
Top of the World **70**
tourist information **107**
Tournament of Kings **51**
Toys of Yesteryear **48**
transportation **106–7**

Treasure Island **111**
Tropicana **11, 67, 115**
Comedy Stop **67**
Folies Bergere **11, 67**
Tule Springs **75**

U

University of Nevada **34**

V

Valley of Fire State Park **90–2**
Vegas for the Boys **65–7**
Venetian **36–7, 44, 50–1, 55, 88, 111, 118**
Bernard Passman Gallery **37**
gondolas **51**
Grand Canal **36, 44, 57**
Guggenheim-Hermitage
Museum **37, 44**
Regis Galerie **36–7**
Very Bad Things **23**
video poker machines **80**
visas **107–8**
Viva Las Vegas **22**
Viva Vision **12, 89**

W

websites **108**
weddings **20–1, 68, 108–9**
weights and measures **109**
white tigers **33**
women **56–9, 109**
Wynn, Steve **25, 29, 36, 40–2, 62**
Wynn Las Vegas **40–1, 47, 62, 65, 111**
Golf and Country Club **65**

X

X Scream (ride) **53**

Z

Zumanity **68, 71**

Pangkor Laut Resort, Malaysia

HotelClub.com

JOIN
THE CLUB!

Earn Rewards, Get Discounts,
Stay Free, Only with HotelClub!
Across 30,000 Hotels in
120 Countries

£10
OFF
see reverse for details

INSIGHT GUIDES
www.insightguides.com

Register with
HotelClub.com
and get £10!

At *HotelClub.com*, we reward our Members with
discounts and free stays in their favourite hotels. As
a Member, every booking made by you through
HotelClub.com will earn you Member Dollars.

When you register, we will credit your Member Account
with *£10* Member Dollars* – which you can use on your next
HotelClub.com booking. Log on to *www.HotelClub.com/
stepguide* to activate your *HotelClub.com* Membership.
Complete your details, including the Membership Number &
Password located on the back of the *HotelClub.com* card.

Over 5 million Members already use Member Dollars to pay for
all or part of their hotel bookings. Join now and start spending
Member Dollars whenever and wherever you want – you are
not restricted to specific hotels or dates!

With great savings of up to 60% on over 30,000 hotels across
120 countries, you are sure to find the perfect location for
business or pleasure. Happy travels from *HotelClub.com!*

* Equivalent to USD $17. One Member Dollar = USD $1

www.insightguides.com